EVERY FURY ON EARTH

Every fury on earth has been absorbed in time,
as art, or as religion, or as authority in one form or another.
The deadliest blow the enemy of the human soul can strike is
to do fury honor.

—James Agee

EVERY FURY ON EARTH

JOHN H. SUMMERS

The PenMark Press
The Davies Group, Publishers
Aurora CO 80044-0140 USA

The PenMark Press, an imprint of
The Davies Group, Publishers
PO Box 440140
Aurora CO 80044-0140, USA

Library of Congress Cataloging-in-Publication Data

Summers, John H., 1971-
  Every fury on earth / John H. Summers.
    p. cm.
  ISBN-13: 978-1-934542-07-1 (alk. paper)
  ISBN-10: 1-934542-07-5 (alk. paper)
  1. United States--Intellectual life--20th century. 2. Intellectuals--United States--History--20th century. 3. Intellectuals--United States--Biography. 4. United States--Social conditions--20th century. I. Title.
  E169.12.S868 2008
  001.10973'0904--dc22
                              2008038519

Editor: The Davies Group, Editors
Interior Design: The Davies Group, Designers
Cover Art: The Louis Orr etching of Widener Library (1936) is
         reproduced by permission of Harvard University Archives,
         call #UAV 827.5, Box 8, "Engraving" folder. The font used
         is Engravers MT.
Printed on acid-free paper

For Daniel Moses

A NOTE TO THE READER

For inspired conversation and moral aid, I thank Todd Gitlin, Claire Lewis, Daniel Moses, George Scialabba, Anna Summers, Cathy Tumber, Robert Westbrook, and Alan Wolfe.

I am grateful to The Davies Group for turning these essays, most of which were orphaned in magazines and newspapers, into a singular volume.

TABLE OF CONTENTS

FOREWORD

The essays in this volume vary in length from one thousand to ten thousand words. In subject, they vary from trends in higher education to the histories of sex scandals and dreaming in American politics; from the radical left in San Francisco to the utopian ego driving information technology; from the intellectual biographies of James Agee and Richard Hofstadter to Christopher Hitchens and C. Wright Mills. No one theme or person or subject dominates. Although the essays are in spirit critical, they do not advance the interests of any party or group or milieu.

I invite readers to regard the essays as the result of a sensibility that wants to make knowledge available for intellectual self-defense. In this regard, the subjects selected themselves, each of them having puzzled, angered, or startled me in the decade since 1998 when I began writing for publication. I had turned away from the rural conservatism of my youth, which held violence and tradition to be the motors of history, only to find myself superfluous, delivered neither to the Old Left nor the New Left, but, instead, to no Left at all. Becoming radically aware of politics and culture in the Age of Reagan absolved me of the old cycle of illusion and disillusion, but only because there were no longer any illusions on offer, no ideologies or clear standards of political belief by which to measure myself.

How, then, is it possible to believe in the transcendent or progressive power of ideas while disbelieving in authority? This is the question presented in the epigraph and featured in the title. I hope that, in bringing the question to bear on these subjects, I have not taken the easy way out.

I

HISTORY AS VOCATION

HISTORY AS VOCATION

Although I was born and raised in Gettysburg, my interest in history consisted of scouting the battlefield for patches of land where my friends and I could swill beer without attracting the park rangers. The only evidence that I possessed books lies in my memory of using them to light the bonfire at our high school graduation party.

Not until I moved to Washington D.C., following a lackluster performance at college in rural Virginia, did I decide to take evening classes in the master's program at George Mason University. There I met Roy Rosenzweig, who introduced me to academic history and encouraged me in all the ways that count for a young man enduring his first ecstasies of learning without a background in higher education. Led by Roy and Lawrence Levine, who had recently migrated from Berkeley, George Mason's History Department was staffed by a crew of assistant professors hip to the literary theory then in fashion. Had I entered the academy with Roy, twenty years earlier, I might have taken my training in social history. I might have tried to relate my discoveries to a social movement outside the university. Social history, sociology, and social movements, however, had exhausted their innovations by the nineties. Cultural Studies had replaced them as a source of radical political speculation across the humanities. The result was bracing. I went from burning books to describing them as "cultural artifacts."

I quit my job and went full-time. Roy was the hub. He saw in new technology a means to consolidate and distribute the gains social history had made. He worked closely with Steve Brier and Josh Brown at the American Social History Project (ASHP) at the Graduate

Center, City University of New York. Having struck up a synthesis with the textbook *Who Built America?*, they had transformed the first volume into a multimedia cd-rom. I signed on as research assistant for the second volume and had a hand in minor projects for years thereafter. The solidarity was engrossing. Roy founded the Center for History and New Media several months after I began classes. He built it from a sheet of paper tacked to his office door into one of the world's leading centers of its kind.

■■■

My studies at George Mason culminated in a conventional paper on Dale Carnegie's *How to Win Friends and Influence People*. Even this modest exercise, however, illustrated the world of contrasts that opened between my past and my choice of vocation. *Who Built America?* identified the history of the country with the history its working-class. As the son and grandson of small businessmen, I grew up despising labor unions. That most of my professors were not only pro-labor radicals, but *Jewish* radicals, disclosed aspects of culture (and reality) that my upbringing had ignored or denied. In my family, moreover, *How to Win Friends and Influence People* ranked with the great documents of the twentieth century, slightly above Russell Conwell's "Acres of Diamonds" and Andrew Carnegie's "The Gospel of Wealth."

My family members—teachers, nurses, and small business-men—inhabited the hamlets of Adams County, Pennsylvania, as self-conscious descendents of conservative German and English farmers. We have been living in the area since the eighteenth century. The county has voted Republican in every presidential election since 1920 (including the election of 2004). Ronald Reagan was a culture hero as well as a political leader. Now it is George Bush who moves them.

All along they have paid out large sums to attend the Dale Carnegie Institute, at once affirming their ideological inheritance of Protestant individualism and adapting it to the realities of the modern corporation. In my final paper I criticized Carnegie as the Machiavelli of the *petite bourgeoisie*. They applauded Carnegie's ingenuity in defending American capitalism against communists, hippies, queers, blacks, Jews, Jesse Jackson, and Jane Fonda.

The radical social movements that had shaped Roy Rosenzweig's youth in Queens never visited my part of rural Pennsylvania, not even when they were most needed. "Many servicemen in Vietnam feel that when they are sent over here it is for a duty that they themselves cannot fully understand and thus will not give their complete cooperation," my father had written from somewhere in Southeast Asia, in a letter published in the local newspaper in December 1970. Earlier that summer, having gone eagerly into a war that was already lost, he had found himself fighting a rearguard battle against his fellow Marines. In his letter, he traced variations in their morale to the varying political attitudes of their home communities. The quality of his own patriotism he brandished proudly. "Being over here is not a duty to me, but rather a privilege—a chance to help our great country in whatever way I can, also a chance to give something back to the community which has helped me in so many fine ways."

My father left Saigon with an injured leg, a Purple Heart, and nobility intact. The meaning of his sacrifice he had determined before he went. If any one book caused me to enroll in George Mason, it was Neil Sheehan's *A Bright Shining Lie*, which I read almost by accident after college. At home, broaching any such discussion of the morality of the war's aims provoked the furies. Vietnam, thus understood, invigilated my adolescence as the Lost Cause once affected southern youth. There was the same intimate connection between history and biography on display; the same embattled refusal to confront the toll of a mistaken war; the same odor of unconfessed shame. At sixteen, watching the Iran-Contra hearings on television with my grandfather, I donated a portion of my summer wages to Colonel Oliver North's defense fund. By the time I left George Mason a decade later I had renounced my patrimony and embraced my re-baptism, without, however, knowing where it might lead.

▙▙▙

I cannot believe any doctoral program in the country afforded greater freedom to think through such matters than the Department of

History at the University of Rochester, where I enrolled in 1996. The faculty there drew no firm line between the practice of history, journalism, and social science because they rejected the modern graduate school's invidious distinction between scholarship and citizenship. They never discouraged graduate students from contributing to upmarket magazines and newspapers, nor to the broadest possible range of scholarly journals. I loved it. In addition to completing seminar work in intellectual history, I served as president of the university's Graduate Organizing Group, participated in Rochester Labor Council's Workforce Education Program, hosted Christopher Hitchens, Katha Pollitt, Ralph Nader, and other public figures, and published my first essays.

The generosity entailed by the Department's conception of history as a vocation spared me the assumption, rigorously enforced among the graduate students I began to meet elsewhere, that to achieve success in the field was to drive for disciplinary knowledge. It also spared me the snobbish assumption, increasingly apparent in those same graduate students, that democratic societies cannot generate cultural excellence. Many and varied were the obligations of the aspiring historian, and mastering historiography was high on the list at Rochester, to be sure. The first and most important was landing an argument on the level of abstraction between the specialists and the boobs. Telling them apart was the hardest part.

The legendary personalities in the Department's history still excited interest among the graduate students, encouraging us to honor its legacy of bold, politically active scholarship. Norman O. Brown and Eugene Genovese had taught in the Department. So had Herbert Gutman, co-founder of the American Social History Project and co-author of *Who Built America?* Christopher Lasch had outlasted them all. It was he who made the most appealing model to me. Lasch died two years before I arrived, but his exemplary body of work presided over the Department as a standing challenge. *The New Radicalism in America* helped me to locate myself in a tradition of intellectual revolt against middle-class families and taught me to beware the social isolation to which it often led. *The Culture of Narcissism* and

The True and Only Heaven tutored me in a sensibility aloof from the canting conservatism I once knew and the liberal tradition I might have considered its only alternative.

In the genealogy of radical social thought that focused my attention, no family of ideas was more significant than pragmatism. I learned to respect the relativity of knowledge, to test the value of ideas by their power to influence action, to define inquiry in the vocabulary of naturalism, to associate freedom with "creative intelligence." These lessons collected toward a center in Robert Westbrook's *John Dewey and American Democracy*, the most accomplished book in the Department, at least among those sensitive to its recent political history. Rather than inflating the significance of his subject, Westbrook made Dewey appear less influential than received opinion suggested. Dewey was not *the* representative liberal philosopher of the Progressive Era, though Progressivism established the major context for his work. He was a prophet of democracy whose most radical insights had been scanted, misunderstood, or ignored by his critics. In *The Revolt of the Elites*, Christopher Lasch, one such critic, reversed his judgment of Dewey and dedicated this final book to Westbrook.

"Democracy is neither a form of government nor a social expediency," Dewey once wrote, "but a metaphysic of the relation of man and his experience to nature." With Westbrook as my advisor, I began to see the implications. Democracy was not only procedures and institutions. It was an embattled political theory indebted to theology, as well as to the human sciences. It was a social struggle on the part of movements to improve the quality of community life. It was the main story in the ongoing drama of American power abroad.

As for pragmatism, a revival had been brewing in literary criticism, law, and philosophy since the seventies. But timing is the key to inspiration, and the political entailments of Dewey's pragmatism were never more compelling than in the decade after 1991, when *John Dewey and American Democracy* appeared. Westbrook presented a theoretically sophisticated argument for radical democracy on premises independent of liberal capitalism and Marxist socialism. In the decade after the fall of the Soviet Union, while Marxism was pronounced obsolete and democracy and capitalism were held to be analytically and actually indistinct, to be armed with the Deweyan dissent was immensely useful. Of the dwindling number of leftist radicals I met in Rochester in the late nineties, a handful continued to call themselves Marxists. Few did so without hesitation. The rest could call themselves democrats or anarchists, as I eventually decided to call myself, without flinching.

The choice to write a dissertation about C. Wright Mills came easily. Mills's writings in the forties and fifties made him, chronologically speaking, a key figure in the development of radical social thought from John Dewey to Christopher Lasch. Mills had written his dissertation about Dewey (one of his "godfathers") and Lasch had cited Mills repeatedly and enthusiastically. The disorderly transmission of radical values from generation to generation had puzzled all three men. A study of Mills seemed a good way to repair some broken links and to improve the scattershot and polemical quality of the secondary literature. In *Achieving Our Country* (1998), Richard Rorty accused the "Mills-Lasch thesis" of misleading the New Left on the threat of international communism. Rorty criticized Mills's call for "our own separate peace" with communist intellectuals. But Rorty did not tell readers that Mills had made his call *after* the death of Stalin, during a political moment pregnant with reasons to hope for a détente. Elsewhere, Rorty (mis)attributed the idea of "separate peace" to Lasch.

I thought these casual errors, all-too-common in the literature surrounding Mills, masked his rightful place in the Deweyan tradition that Rorty admired and promoted. Then, too, the emotional and ethical force of Mills's style moved me. After reading *The Power Elite*, I found myself grappling with a genuine biography, not a study of ideas, but a chronicle of a life-in-ideas. Mills claimed that history as a record of presumptive collective action was ending, that the machinery of the "post-modern epoch" was hollowing out the moral culture of democracy. His personal history seemed to tell a more sanguine tale. Born and educated in Texas, he arrived at Columbia University in

1945 as a prince of sociology, winning tenure there before he turned 40. He published 10 books, including four bestsellers in nine years, and experimented with organic farming, architecture, marriage, photography, and motorcycling.

I decided to treat his flamboyant egotism as the instrument of his energies, hoping to engage readers in the most complete possible range of legitimate responses. In "What Makes a Life Significant," William James offered a warrant for this decision. "What our human emotions seem to require is the sight of the struggle going on," James wrote. "The moment the fruits are being merely eaten, things become ignoble. Sweat and effort, human nature strained to its utmost and on the rack, yet getting through alive, and then turning its back on its successes to pursue another more rare and arduous still—this is the sort of thing the presence of which inspires us, and the reality of which seems to be the function of all the higher forms of literature and fine art to bring home to us and suggest." Dead at forty-five, Mills spent his brief life "on the rack."

The challenge is to lash an unusually wide range of subjective judgments onto the objective rigor of historical analysis, to honor the technical standards of scholarship without dishonoring the spiritual qualities that stamp biography with its humanistic bias. How might biographies of charismatic intellectuals heal the wound between the argumentative and evocative dimensions in our literature? How might "force and fire" and "sweetness and light," those dueling motifs in Anglo-American letters, mingle in mutual aid and sympathy?

▌▌▌

A biography of Mills also seemed a good way to explore the history of the academic profession to which I had entrusted myself. Already by the time Herbert Gutman, Eugene Genovese, and Christopher Lasch had converged in the Rochester History Department in the early seventies, several generations of satirists had taken aim at the petty ironies and defrauded ambitions dogging campus society, working in the conflict between liberal education, with its emancipatory ideals, and the vocational ethos of colleges and universities. "We find ourselves uncomfortable in academic life and often at odds with the profession and the university," Lasch wrote in 1973. To read today's satirists alongside the novels that founded the genre in this period is to be struck by the irony of a satire that never quite transcended the object of its mockery.

If the least that could be said for the academic profession in the seventies was that it offered job security, health insurance, and a full-time salary, this was more than subsequent generations had the right to expect. The job market collapsed. The last person who believed it would recover was the economist and higher education expert William G. Bowen, President of Princeton University until 1988, when he became President of the Andrew W. Mellon Foundation. The next year, in an annual report widely paraphrased and disseminated to college students, myself included, Bowen at once overlooked the biggest story in graduate education and helped to exacerbate its worst features. "The immediate pressures on our graduate schools to provide faculty members for colleges and universities will be considerable in the 1990s," he wrote. "The results of recent research persuade us that there will be serious staffing problems in essentially all fields within the arts and sciences." Bowen predicted "very substantial [faculty] shortages" in the humanities and social sciences, such that, by the late nineties, "the competition for faculty members could become so acute that it would threaten the quality of teaching and research in all of higher education."

Legions of students took Bowen's advice into graduate school and learned to sight the trouble from the opposite direction. University managers applied to the academic profession the downsizing and outsourcing techniques perfected by the corporations. Neither the political history of this purge, nor its cumulative effect on intellectual freedom, was well understood at the time. In 1998, in conjunction with the Rochester Labor Council, I co-organized a one-day conference on the changing nature of academic work and came away impressed by the meagerness of our collective understanding. Apparently, I was not alone in finding it difficult to comprehend how ruthlessly the life of the mind could be made the prey of market forces. *Academic labor?*

Could the scholar's natural rights to contradiction and spontaneity obey an industrial discipline? If those rights were alienated, would not the qualities of mind they represent wither in their turn?

The University of Rochester was led by Thomas Jackson, a bankruptcy attorney by training and spirit. Of the bad ideas Jackson and his minions promulgated, none affected me more directly than their decision to institute a writing program for the benefit of the "customers," i.e., the undergraduates. Curriculum-wide composition programs are notoriously expensive to administer and laborious to teach. The Jackson administration, finding graduate students the cheapest and most convenient solution, thus conscripted us into service. The terms of our fellowships shifted, the decision made by administrative fiat. To continue to receive our stipends we would have to interrupt our studies and teach remedial writing. I gave the course once, then left the rest of the money on the table, moving to Austin to work in the C. Wright Mills papers at the University of Texas.

▌▌▌

Over the next three years, 1999 to 2002, I served as graduate-student representative to the American Historical Association's first Committee on Part-Time and Adjunct Employment. In this same period I founded and edited a column on graduate education in the AHA's newsletter, *Perspectives*. Here, as elsewhere, I argued that if history was a craft then historians should organize themselves into guilds and strive for independence from the point of production. A guild, so conceived, regulates admission to its ranks; enforces the ethical and aesthetic standards of its craft against the pecuniary interests of employers; multiplies classes and types of jobs in sympathy with the skills and desires of its membership.

Organizations such as the American Historical Association, which present themselves as custodians of the standards by which scholars are educated, accredited, and employed, bear a passing resemblance to the guild ideal. Yet professors in America have never formed such self-governing bodies *and* invested them with necessary economic powers and political responsibilities. As a result, the young scholar has been defenseless, confronted by insultingly narrow job descriptions and forced to transmit knowledge by paraphrase, in prefabricated, digestible forms and methods easily copied. Then the demands made upon the successful teacher establish the criteria for legitimate research. Promotion means proving one's competence by writing a thesis-driven monograph in one small corner of one small field. Tenure means retaining responsibility for it, and often for it alone, forever after.

Most literate adults could master professional history's dozen Big Ideas in a long summer of reading the state-of-the- field handbooks. Could they *read* the dissertations and monographs, which hang like edicts over the souls of scholars? The graduate student or assistant professor bores into a mass of dumb facts with tools handed down by forebears, then *deposits* the product in the library-bank for reference and storage; but not often for reading.

As a permanent class of lecturers and adjunct teachers took shape in the nineties, it fell to a new group of union organizers to establish a measure of independence over the point of academic production. In return, they generated a vicious opposition from the most powerful faculties in the country, although these faculties have had little to offer but a restatement of their privileges. And from the rest? The plight of the scholar who once expected to command a seller's market elicited vested indifference or outright incomprehension. Professors have continued to think of themselves as craftsman even as they fulfilled the economic functions of corporate managers and bosses. Rochester historians bemoaned the divestment of upstate New York, where disappearing manufacturing jobs stranded thousands of unemployed and unemployable workers. Yet these same historians baulked before their complicity in a system of graduate education that wasted its products by similar dynamics of over-production and under-employment.

Who is responsible? Nobody can say. The losers are referred to The Market. That they are so referred by the same professors who have built careers on criticizing the irrationality of unregulated markets—everywhere except in their own departments—has made the news all the more difficult to bear.

My experience with the American Historical Association suggested a collective inability on the part of professors to act. The discussions of the Committee on Part-Time and Adjunct Employment taught me that, with some exceptions, the leading members of the AHA are convinced of their helplessness. They might affirm the right of teaching assistants to form unions, but they would not bring the fight for full-time, benefits-eligible work to the accrediting agencies, where power lies. Nor would they tolerate much impudence. After sixteen months of editing "Issues in Graduate Education," in which I made readers of *Perspectives* eat a steady diet of protest and analysis, I was instructed to moderate the message. I resigned instead, and was replaced by a cadre of graduate students who set about commissioning articles on the best layout for curriculum vitae, and other Significant Subjects.

▌▌▌

The intellectual fragmentation of the humanities has undermined the ability of their spokespeople to mount a common defense of the very idea of a free professional, with rights and values distinct from the mere employee. Yet the social life of professionalism persists. Critics who voice their arguments from outside the cool, detached register of academic argument meet epigrams aimed at dissuasion such as *pick your battles* (a euphemism for do not fight *this* battle) and maxims against *burning bridges* (as if bridges built upon a suspension of one's critical faculties might lead anywhere one might wish to go).

Within these broad limits I have struggled, no doubt unsuccessfully, to reduce the bombast in my writing. *Some* bombast appears to be inevitable. If the political psychology of righteous indignation is too prominent among anarchists, that is because our method of locating responsibility for suffering outside immediate experience continually risks blurring distinctions between I and other, self and society. Anarchism has no philosophy of history, no superannuated system of concepts to blunt the knife-edge of personal complaints. Criticism turns to querulous resentments. "Every poor devil finds pleasure in scolding," Nietzsche wrote of the anarchist temper. "It gives him a little of the intoxication of power. There is a small dose of *revenge* in every complaint. On the basis of this logic one makes revolutions." Then again, without punishment there is no culture, even if the antithesis (without culture there is only punishment) is also true. The resolution, if there is one, should lie in the critic's cultivation of distinctions between blame and pique, justice and revenge. The facility for keeping them in view must come out of radical self-awareness and self-discipline.

The dissuaders flee from the risks and burdens of engaged criticism by taking shelter in a ready-made hierarchy of values; or, they absolve the ugliness of public life into the old Mugwump gentility, warning against *being negative* because they believe conflict inflicts psychic damage. Either they withdraw into an absolutist morality; or they withdraw into a nihilism that cowers before the task of judgment because it cannot imagine any values worth defending. The alternative, the Dale Carnegie way, skirts the whole problem. "When dealing with people, remember you are not dealing with creatures of logic, but creatures of emotion," Carnegie says. "The only way to get the best of an argument is to avoid it." Touché.

On the campus itself, the professional tone is still available to those who would insulate themselves from criticism over values. Governed by committees and rituals of dissent, the professor beholds a morally passionate challenge as little more than heckling. The erosion of the economic basis of middle-class professionalism might have disturbed the quietism in the professional manner if it had not found support from an unexpected source in what Lynn Hunt has called "the feminization of history" and humanities teaching. American women in the nineteenth century seized control over the primary schools with a thoroughness unknown in any other part of the world. Since the last formal barriers to women faculty fell in the seventies, they have achieved comparably disproportionate gains in universities. That their achievement has coincided with a decline in the status of college teaching and a partial withdrawal of the jobs from the full economy lies within the historical norm in America. Has the feminization of campus society also inculcated a sentimental attitude toward students?

Has it inculcated a political correctness that causes criticism to die on the tongue?

Carnegie promised white-collar men that if they emasculated themselves—if they suppressed their instinct for conflict by eliding the distinction between sincerity and the performance of sincerity—then success would be theirs. Feminization offers the same bargain by a pedagogy of therapeutic uplift and ego-building. I am not sure how one might demonstrate this. When I began teaching at Harvard University I know that more than half my colleagues were women, and I thought I saw feminization omnipresent. Toward the end, when President Larry Summers lost his job and was replaced by Drew Faust, a woman historian, I thought I saw it running at high tide.

▐▐▐

Arriving at Harvard in the summer of 2000, I joined the staff of the Committee on Degrees in Social Studies, the fifth largest concentration in the College and the most distinguished of its honors programs. As Tutor, then as Lecturer, I advised senior theses, conceived and conducted freshman and junior seminars, and taught the sophomore tutorial six times. The fractured nature of my appointment, renewed annually for six successive years while never amounting to more than 65 percent in any one year, kept me on the margins of prestige and promotion even as it kept me there long enough to serve three Chairpersons of Social Studies and two Directors of Study.

The position afforded an exhilarating scope of intellectual engagement. I taught the classics of modern European thought, Hobbes to Habermas. Founded in 1960 to combat the fragmentation of liberal arts education, the Committee on Degrees in Social Studies (*not* Social Sciences) had taken its name in the bold spirit of C. Wright Mills's *The Sociological Imagination*. It was an ideal place to study.

It was not an ideal place to teach. The Committee had no ladder faculty of its own. It borrowed assistant professors and staffed its remainders with lecturers and teaching assistants. The students faced a permanent, unavailable faculty on the one hand, and a transient, available class of adjuncts on the other. The fragmented composition of the teaching staff continually subverted the committee's interdisciplinary ideals. With no possibility of promotion within Social Studies, the assistant professors and lecturers had to prove themselves in their disciplines, where tenure waited at the edge of their thoughts. A colleague once explained to me that although Social Studies gave equal time to Michel Foucault and Jurgen Habermas, assistant professorships in political theory split between "Foucaultians" and "Habermasians." One had to choose. Rather than encouraging a transvaluation of academic methods and disciplines, as the founders intended, Social Studies trundled from one to the next. Its isolation, in turn, was physically represented by its location on the edge of the campus, far from Harvard Yard.

As an adjunct, I had no job description, no political rights, no promise of renewal beyond each year and thus no basis to protest the opaque manner by which tutorial assignments were decided and distributed. Class consciousness among the adjuncts was nil. The corporate mentality was much in evidence. Accordingly, it was never enough to perform one's duties well. One was expected to attest to the benevolence of the institution. As consumers turn themselves into adjuncts of corporate marketing departments, so adjunct faculty identify their self-worth with the propaganda-interests of their employers. And why not? Everyone recognizes the value of the Harvard Corporation's brand.

I found the students the strangest part of the scene. It was not that their demand for *relevance* vitiated the mission of Social Studies; relevance was always the price that liberal arts have had to pay to gain a place in the curriculum. It was their fetish for wealth and status I found so striking. Harry Lewis, the Dean of Harvard College, described the campus culture as *Excellence Without a Soul* (2006), a harsher phrase than any that crossed my mind. Yet I, too, was startled by the cynicism of the students.

During my time at George Mason, I had sent my parents a copy of "So You Want to be a Historian," an essay in the *Washington Post Education Review*. It described the life of the mind as a calling that demanded not only an heroic commitment to reading and writing, but a spiritual conviction of the importance of knowledge and sensibility freely achieved. I sent the essay home because it explained why I wanted to pursue a life of scholarship. Over the next decade, as religious enthusiasm swept through Gettysburg, the spiritual component of my vocation remained eccentric there. At Harvard, meanwhile, I confronted another form of anti-intellectualism. My interview for the position in Social Studies ended with a warning from the Director of Studies. Never show weakness in the presence of the students, she said, calling them "sharks" and promising they would "eat you alive."

■■■

The post-pubescents of notables for whom I suddenly found myself holding curricular responsibility included the daughter of a U.S. Senator, the son of a Hollywood director, and the son of New Jersey real-estate developer Charles Kushner, named here because he is a leading example in Daniel Golden's piquant *The Price of Admission*. Not long before Mr. Kushner was indicted for bribery (he was convicted on tax charges) he got his son Jared into Harvard by a $2.5 million donation. Back in prep school (according to Mr. Golden), Jared had not impressed his teachers or guidance counselors as the kind of student who might excel academically. Of this curious background I knew nothing at the first meeting of my first seminar of my first year, when Jared entered my classroom and promptly took the seat across from mine, sharing the room, so to speak. I was drawing an annual salary of $15,500, and borrowing the remainder for required for survival in the Cambridge housing market, in order that Jared might be given the best possible education. I was subsidizing him.

Most of the students I encountered had already embraced the perspectives of the rich, the powerful, and the unalienated, and they seemed to have done so with appalling ease. In keeping with the tradition of the American rich, they worked exceptionally long hours, they were aggressive in exercising their talents, and on the ideological features of market-capitalism they were unanimous. Their written work disclosed the core components of the consensus upheld by their liberal parents: wherever equality of opportunity presents itself, equality of welfare is likely to ensue; the meaning of liberty lies in the personal choice of consumers; free competition in goods and morals regulates value; technological progress is an unmixed good; war is unfortunate.

Around this consensus crystallized an ethos. One of my less affluent students, the son of a postman, asked me for advice about a financial investment. His friends had told him to invest his savings "in prisons"—actually in one of the new private companies gaining management contracts over correctional facilities. Only later, when I learned that his savings totaled a meager $2,000, did I think I understood the pressure he felt. No amount of money may be permitted to lie idle if something may be gotten for nothing. The capitalist theory of life as a game disallows uncapitalized advantages.

I asked the students in each of my seminars whether they had so far encountered a teacher they genuinely appreciated. What aspects of manner did they admire? Invariably the students replied that good teachers made them "feel comfortable." To sense the sterility one had only to listen. When I proposed to teach a junior seminar entitled Anarchist Cultural Criticism in America, I was instructed to go ahead only after I changed the title to America and Its Critics. Here was the same method of cultural hygiene which has transformed Harvard Square from a bohemian enclave into an outdoor mall. "Shopping period" was the name of the week the students select classes.

Grading, the one instrument of power I wielded, offers the best example of the degradation of pedagogy by the frenzy of success. The *Boston Globe*'s expose of grade inflation at Harvard left little doubt that it is a semi-rigged competition, another subsidized risk. The formal scale runs from A to F. The tacit scale runs from A to B. I learned the latter from students and supervisors, but especially from colleagues, few of whom wish to carry the opprobrium of the low end. This is as it may be. But the presence of two standards of value, one official and one tacit, is always a sign of corruption. The one necessarily dishonors the other. It also abridges academic freedom. Although I never dared to give a final grade below B minus, I can attest to the petty harassment that teachers attract in such cases. I do not mean merely that the students are never so aggressive and articulate as when they hunt for grades. I mean they wage political reprisals against the B minus grader and send gifts to high-placed academic directors. Electronic mail abets grade-jockeying by abolishing what little remains of the presumptive moral distance between teachers and students.

In January 2008, a "Group of Harvard Alumni from the Vietnam War Era" sent an open letter to the university's president. "We are concerned by what we see to be the widespread apathy and political indifference of the student body at Harvard College today," said the letter, which defined the problem as "self-examination and broad intellectual growth versus the careerist, vocational orientation." The letter was only half-right: the students are the opposite of apathetic and indifferent. The new student rich has retained the radical energy of the sixties, only to engage it in lushly monetized competencies. The New Left occupied universities to protest the bureaucratic hollowness of examination rituals and grading rationales. Today, its children complete the attack on the authority of teachers, who are simply annexed to the management of student careers, drawn into an agreement between corporation and client in which failure is not an option. I *had* to grade the students, and I had to grade them *well*. *Everyone* expected a recommendation letter.

The ethos mimics the psychodynamics of inflation in this age of unlimited markets. Apparently, since the students were young their parents and teachers have bathed them in ambitious glances, so that the source of their identity has come to lie in their *potential*. This is why, though they demand to be graded, they resent the teacher's claim to judgment based on performance, which implies a stable set of values. A relatively low judgment may be met by the always available thought that they *could have* done better.

This thought is not as easy to rebut as one might suppose. Harvard students may be divided into three types: those who infer from their presence on campus that they have already made it; and those who infer that they are on their way to making it. Both types are keenly aware of the prestige-value of their situation. To mention to a stranger where one attends college is to drop the H-Bomb. Neither type, accordingly, has encountered any really good reason to suppose that their potential is anything but limitless. Members of the third type, the ironists and the scoffers, have their degree and eat it too. Their anti-Harvard posturing incurs no risk. The gigantic endowment, that symbol of unspent potential, blesses their skepticism by indexing their value on the credentials market. Consider that the grading scandal (an open secret on campus) broke into the public discussion at the same time the dot.com bubble burst. Try to see these phenomena as twin instances in the chronic overextension of the credit markets. When scholars act as clerks and students act as clients, college teachers do not differ from corporate accountants.

■■■

If youth is wasted on the young, is teaching wasted on students? And what about the scholar? What happens to those of us who discover a jealous passion when we discover our calling, then find the university, the only institution formally dedicated to upholding the scholarly ideal, unmindful of our aspirations and sedulously banal in its own? "Every young man who feels called to scholarship has to realize clearly that the task before him has a double aspect," Max Weber wrote. "He must qualify not only as a scholar, but also as a teacher. And the two do not at all coincide." The gap between the moral culture of scholarship and the vulgarity of college teaching deserves to be drawn sharply, if only so that it may be mitigated.

To hope for reform, however, is to be fooled twice. The proliferation of ancillary services and the growing power of student affairs offices indicate all trends running in the direction of consumer services. They have been running that way for quite some time. As the sentimentalization of manners has taken feminine form in the professional ethos, so the art of pedagogy has become a service-class preoccupation whose chief duty is flattering students on their way to monied careers. Vain is the image of the college teacher as a bearer of culture, a representative of a value-standard, a model of aspiration and achievement, unapproachable except by knowledgeable respect.

"The great historians, with few exceptions, are those who have not merely studied, but lived; and whose subjects have ranged over a much wider field than the period or subject of which they write." This passage, from Samuel Eliot Morison's *History as a Literary Art: An Appeal to Young Historians*, is full of unfashionable wisdom. I think Morison, in urging scholars to come out of the classroom, meant to protect their drive for self-perfection from the constant company of the very errors only recently left behind. Teaching, so understood, is a form of sabotage. "Every teacher acquires a continually increasing stationary force, a cumulative inertia in proportion to the eloquence of his innovating doctrines," Emerson complained to his journal in 1834. Emerson was one of a surprising number of thinkers who have exerted a pronounced influence on modern thought without ever holding a regular college or university appointment, surprising since colleges and universities are virtually the only places where his influence peeks through. Perhaps he retained his faith in education because the Lyceum was the social setting for his pedagogy. He addressed *his* pupils, *his* public, inspired souls in the garden of *his* perceptions.

Should I say that I am grateful for the chance to teach at Harvard? I am. Should I acknowledge the many fine exceptions it was my privilege to instruct? I do, with pleasure. At the end, however, I made my assignations in the mists. We were all drugged. Teaching on the temporary staff at Harvard was a little like visiting Disneyworld. The magic dust induced a light narcosis. The mind went incontinent in the presence of paradox and conflict, and it was tough to tell how much fun I was having from how much fun I pretending to have. The most important thing was never to become the screamer who ruins the ride for everyone. The line is long.

THE HITCHENS EFFECT

For a few days in November 1997, telephone calls screamed into the office of the president of the University of Rochester. Local television stations and newspapers sounded the alarm of community outrage. University administrators called emergency meetings in which they mobilized the campus security forces, rehearsed plans A and B, and recruited plain-clothed police officers for strategic deployment. What accounted for the uproar? Something, it seemed, to perturb dispositions both heavenly and earthly: Christopher Hitchens had been invited to criticize Mother Teresa.

As the organizer of the event, I had been warned to expect trouble. I had asked Hitchens to speak about his 1995 book, *The Missionary Position: Mother Teresa in Theory and Practice*. With her recent death, it seemed a fine time to hear his views, which looked with cold detachment upon the legacy of Calcutta's Nobel Laureate. I knew that Hitchens believed Mother Teresa had been a "thieving, fanatical dwarf," a "right-wing demagogue," and a dissimulating fraud.

The Missionary Position made devastating allegations, most of which had been ignored by the media. Hitchens challenged Mother Teresa's belief that "poverty is a gift from God." He disputed her contention that abortion and contraception are moral equivalents. He asked why she had cavorted with the leaders of murderous regimes in Haiti, Albania, and Guatemala. Why had she traded favors with the swindler Charles Keating? The press in Calcutta had written scathing obituaries, accusing her of leaving little more than hunger and exploitation. Other than proselytization, what had she accomplished with the tens of millions of dollars that had come her way? Hitchens was asking hard questions about philanthropy, poverty, celebrity, and religion. Here was iconoclasm at its best.

The advertisements for the lecture attracted some interest on campus. But this was overshadowed by the "community outrage" manufactured by Gannett's *Democrat and Chronicle*, the city's largest, most influential, and indeed only daily newspaper. What did the *D&C* tell its readers about Christopher Hitchens? Almost nothing worthwhile. Along with local television stations, it reduced the meaning of the coming lecture to a set of vocabulary words, then repeated them *ad nauseum*: "abortion," "atheist," "controversy."

Three days before the lecture, the *D&C* announced on page one that Catholics were "enraged" at the impending speech and reported that a protest of "perhaps more than 200 people" was afoot. In fact, the threat of protest was the work of a small number of anti-abortionists who called themselves The Lambs of Christ. They planned to bus in protestors from the surrounding region. Many churchgoers seemed open to the idea of a fresh perspective on this issue. They included Bishop Matthew Clark, who insisted that universities were obligated to entertain dissenting viewpoints—hardly an "enraged" comment.

The *D&C* turned the lecture into an event, then into a lurid melodrama: an insolent atheist would speak at the university, offending all Catholics while furnishing nothing of substance to a properly hostile public.

▪▪▪

The coverage following the lecture was dominated by depictions of the protests: colorful photos of middle-aged co-religionists standing athwart with lighted candles. Less than 60 had turned out, about 150 fewer "enraged Catholics" than the *D&C* had predicted. The coverage, moreover, lost sight of all the nuances in the lecture itself, attributing to Hitchens a pro-abortion agenda even though he explicitly confessed his ambivalence on this issue; it was Mother Teresa's conflation of contraception and abortion to which he objected.

The newspaper's most egregious offense against truth appeared in an editorial on November 12. Though it purported to be a stiff rejoinder to Hitchens, it bore hardly any relation to the ideas expressed either in his speech or in his book. I phoned the author for an explanation. In the course of our conversation he said that: (1) He had not attended the lecture; (2) He had neither read Hitchens' book nor viewed the accompanying documentary; (3) Before Hitchens came to town, he had never heard of him; and (4) He claimed no particular expertise or insight into the meaning of Mother Teresa's life. I expressed my surprise. He declined to concede that there was anything wrong with the editorial.

▬▬▬

Was controversy inevitable? Probably. Then again, what if the local media had faithfully communicated Hitchens' criticisms of Mother Teresa? What if they had trusted their readers to digest and assimilate unpleasant ideas? The city's smaller, independent news outlets did just that. The *Catholic Courier,* the diocese's own weekly, dispensed a truthful and fair-minded accounting of the lecture. It summoned an expert on Mother Teresa for an earnest refutation, but the piece left no doubt about the merits of Hitchens' analysis and was refreshingly absent of hagiography.

The alternative weekly, *City Paper,* linked Hitchens' evaluation of religious fundamentalism with the larger problem of charity, as did a local public radio program, which allocated him nearly a full hour of airtime. This program elicited a single recalcitrant caller, against more than a dozen respectful questioners. This was no surprise to Hitchens, who insisted that thoughtful people greet him virtually everywhere his work is treated with care.

Despite the negative publicity and the accompanying calls for a boycott, nearly 500 people filled the auditorium. Hitchens and his audience—some from campus, some from the community—debated complex matters like idolatry in a secular society and the politics of poverty. Nearly everyone was well behaved. The participants, by no means all convinced, nonetheless seemed to appreciate Hitchens' forthright judgments, as well as his willingness to consider their disagreements. They stayed for more than three hours.

Hitchens' prior appearance at Johns Hopkins University suggests the same dynamics elsewhere. When word of his visit reached Baltimore's conservative Catholics, reports Mark Crispin

Miller—noted media critic and director of the film series in which Hitchens was scheduled to appear—Archbishop William H. Keeler and his conservative flock reacted in an "explosion of indignation." Keeler organized a campaign of angry phone calls, threatened a protest, and denounced the entire affair as a simple-minded attack on the faithful. Like the *D&C* in Rochester, the *Baltimore Sun* smeared Hitchens on its front page.

The efforts of Keeler and the *Sun,* however, failed badly. The event generated an "astonishing turnout," says Miller. As for the protest, Miller told me that it was a "pathetic demonstration," attracting few of the churlish callers that had earlier besieged him and his sponsors. Most pathetic, perhaps, was the *Sun's* attempt at redemption. After the lecture, the Times-Mirror-owned paper now called the Hitchens visit a "blow for freedom of expression."

THE TOUGHEST JOB

Once every generation, businessmen, journalists, and college officials join English professors in a chorus of lament about the state of literacy. According to the "Johnny Can't Write" refrain—made popular by *Newsweek* in the 1970s—students in the United States cannot recognize elementary standards of grammar. An assessment by the Lehman Brothers investment firm renewed this long-held sentiment in 1996. "Businesses," noted the report, "complain that they cannot employ the 'product' coming out of our schools because graduates cannot read and write, and, recognizing the consequences of this situation in the context of a global economy, businesses are demanding immediate reform."

Complain in this manner about poor writing skills among American undergraduates and the custodians of the literary tradition will wince in knowing assent. Mention Freshman Composition and watch them duck and run, but not before drafting others into the job. Johnny comes to campus and finds his composition course staffed not by an English professor, but by a member of a poorly paid, exploited, and ill-trained underclass of instructors. Confronted by what the *Chronicle of Higher Education* called a "labor crunch" in 1998, administrators across the nation pressed into service scores of graduate students from fields like English and History. No problem? They also took teaching assistants from Musicology and Kinesiology. Few of the conscripts received adequate preparation.

That scandal was noteworthy only for its scale. Non-tenure-line faculty have long carried the burden of the much-despised freshman writing course. According to the National Council of Teachers of English (NCTE), tenured and tenure-track professors staff fewer than five percent of all first-year college writing classes in the United

States. Graduate teaching assistants account for fifty-five percent, and
part-timers and full-time adjuncts another twenty percent each. Writing teachers comprise the largest, oldest, and most abused contingent
of non-tenured instructors in higher education. No other group of
pedagogues has endured so lowly a station for so long. Why does a
society that claims to value writing consign its writing teachers to a
subservient position in the hierarchy of higher learning?

■■■

The history of the problem begins in the nineteenth century, when
a confluence of events simultaneously gave birth to the freshman
composition course and dispatched its instructors to the lowest rungs
of education. By the Gilded Age, silent inscription had displaced
public oratory as a hallmark of advanced thinking; the prestige of the
emerging academic disciplines and the enlightenment of the growing
middle class depended more than ever on the dissemination of printed
scholarship. As rhetoric lost authority to written composition in the
last half of the century, the traditional oral component of the college
curriculum gave way to the freshman writing course.

In 1874, Harvard became the first college to ask its applicants for
a writing sample in English. More than half the candidates turned in
unacceptable performances, and the first of many such crises ensued.
A decade later Harvard's president, Charles W. Eliot, undertook to
remedy the problem by introducing freshman composition into the
curriculum. Every major university soon copied his innovation. Since
its widespread adoption in the late 1880s, composition has enjoyed an
unbroken history in the academy. It remains one of the few courses
that nearly every American college student encounters.

Then, as now, a difficult question confounded the freshman
course: Who would teach it? A few leading scholars—the University of Michigan's Fred Newton Scott, for example—treated it with
intellectual seriousness and plunged dutifully into the business of
teaching writing. Most others evaded it. Francis Child, who occupied
Harvard's distinguished Boylston Chair in Rhetoric from 1851 to
1876, often complained about the amount of time he squandered
correcting undergraduate compositions. Professor Child once punted

a chair across his classroom to protest his compositional obligations. His migration to Johns Hopkins University in 1876 owed much to his determination to avoid any more. In turn, the freshman course's notoriety owed much to Child's widely discussed defection.

To what did Child and the others object? Overwork. Those who ventured into the college writing classroom faced what critic Robert Connors has termed a "nightmare of overwork." In the mid-1890s, four instructors and two graduate students at the University of Michigan wrestled with more than 1,000 students. Twenty teachers evaluated papers for 2,000 undergraduates at Harvard, where Barren Wendell personally graded 24,000 themes every year. Similar situations developed at Yale, Wellesley, Minnesota, Iowa, and other universities, thanks both to high enrollments and to the *laboratory* method, which still makes composition an exceptionally *laborious* course. In a series of reports compiled in 1923 for the NCTE, Edwin Hopkins, a faculty member at the University of Kansas, stressed the difficulty. Hopkins reported that an alarming proportion of writing instructors "certify to wearing out, suffering from nervous exhaustion, loss of efficiency, impaired eyesight, shattered nerves, and collapse — all as the result of attempting to carry a 'killing' overload of pupils in English composition."

The excessive work helps to explain the refusal of the professoriate. Nearly everyone preferred "the glorious liberty of literature." Yet this explanation does not account for the contempt heaped upon the course and its instructors. Literature was easier to teach, but why did the leading members of English departments treat composition as a subservient branch of learning and writing instructors as an underclass? "The opinion that the correcting of school compositions is a low and disagreeable form of mental labor has been expressed so often and with so much emphasis and by so many eminent authorities that it has now come to be regarded as part of the condensed wisdom of humanity," noted Fred Newton Scott in 1903. "During the years of his training the instructor-to-be has not only been taught composition, but he has been led to regard the work as dull, uninteresting," Lyle Spencer noted a decade later. "He has been taught, if not by precept, certainly by example, that composition teaching is menial work, drudgery, a pursuit to be avoided."

How did composition acquire its invidious trappings? In the modern era—the "predatory phase of life," as Thorstein Veblen called it—particular kinds of labor take on the attribute of "irksomeness." Veblen thought the "assertion of prowess, not of diligence," signifies superior work. Socially valuable labor that involves proximity to tools "carries a taint, and all contamination from vulgar employments must be shunned by self-respecting men." As Veblen elaborated in *The Theory of the Leisure Class* (1899), "conspicuous abstention from labor becomes the mark of superior pecuniary achievement and the conventional index of reputability; and conversely, since application to productive labor is a mark of poverty and subjection, it becomes inconsistent with a reputable standing in the community." So conceived, efforts to denigrate composition as an irksome necessity—while ennobling the study of literature as an honorable enterprise—appear as an assertion of class superiority. Demeaned for their usefulness, composition teachers stand in contrast to the more abstract teaching of literature. Reading, not writing, comprises its cardinal activity; leisure, not labor, its leading connotation.

Literature is still the prize, while the ordeal of correcting themes is still reserved for what Robert Connors calls "a cadre of graduate assistants, low-level instructors, part-timers, and departmental fringe people who have become a permanent composition underclass." Women, in particular, teach the course in numbers disproportionate to their overall presence in higher education. In 1929, thirty-eight percent of all composition teachers were women. (Only home economics had a higher percentage of feminine labor). Today, more than two-thirds of writing instructors are female. Part-timers, non-tenure-line full-timers, and graduate teaching assistants ("men and women of uncertain or negative qualifications," as one literature professor called this class in 1921) still comprise the first line of attack in the composition classroom.

To ask a tenured scholar to shoulder the burden of writing instruction is to violate a fundamental axiom of hierarchy in America's knowledge industry. As Veblen articulated the precept, "the able-bodied barbarian of the predatory culture, who is at all mindful of his good name, leaves all uneventful drudgery to the women and minors of the group. He puts in his time in the manly arts of war and devotes his talents to devising ways and means of disturbing the peace. That way lies honor."

▌▌▌

What is to be done? The last few decades have witnessed the emergence of the "new rhetoric," which has given the field—now called Composition Studies—unprecedented theoretical confidence. But preoccupation with professionalization has yielded little material improvement. Practices fixed early in composition's history—low pay, no job security, few chances for promotion, onerous labor-hours per pupil—are much in evidence in the profession's angst-ridden newsletters. The large numbers of underemployed Ph.D.s in English continues to supply a cheap and demoralized labor pool. Meanwhile, the "new rhetoric" has made Composition Studies as trendy, as over theorized, and as exclusionary as any other field that demands a ritualistic parade of abstruse theory for participation in its journals and conferences.

The field's most important reform began in the late 1980s when a band of insurgents created the Wyoming Resolution. In 1989, the Conference on College Composition and Communication (CCCC)—a professional group formed in 1949 under the auspices of the NCTE—incorporated the resolution into a "Statement of Principles and Standards." The CCCC characterized the situation of its membership as "the worst scandal in higher education today," one that had produced "an enormous academic underclass." The Statement of Principles called for tenured, full-time status for qualified composition teachers; limits on the use of part-time labor; course sections of not more than twenty students; and time to conduct scholarly research and to design individualized syllabi. The CCCC's Statement of Principles won the endorsement of other professional organizations, including the Modern Language Association, and has made the measure of indignities and exploitative practices.

In my view, composition teachers should set aside the issue of professional status and instead join the movement to organize academic labor. Recent campaigns to organize graduate teaching assistants, part-timers, and full-time adjuncts of all disciplines—efforts that have gained momentum and confidence on campuses across the nation—have underscored the idea that nothing motivates universities more effectively than organized action.

Organizing instructors, moreover, would expose the class lines of contemporary higher education. No group of comparable teachers is as large; their potential role in any campus-wide unionization effort is enormous. And they occupy a position in the academy that has long been recognized as useful. In unionization lies the only available strategy for bettering the working lives of writing instructors and the conditions of composition pedagogy.

GRADUATE ECONOMICS

Graduate students at George Washington University staged a spirited public rally at the campus's "Professors Gate" in August 1999. Protesting low wages and a lack of medical benefits, they chanted, "One, two, three, four, GW keeps its teachers poor." At the University of Maryland in College Park, discontented graduate students gathered more than 300 signatures and lobbied the state legislature for the right to form a union. In the 1990s, campaigns like these to organize graduate students into legally recognized unions became almost commonplace. Ten years before, only eight such unions possessed bargaining rights in the United States. By 2000 the number had risen to 22, and a dozen additional campaigns roiled both public and private universities across the nation.

For much of the last century, graduate education hewed closely to the apprenticeship model. A doctoral student took courses, wrote a dissertation and simultaneously learned to teach undergraduates by serving an apprenticeship under a faculty mentor. As an apprentice, or teaching assistant, the student performed a few tasks designed as a long introduction to the craft of education—leading small-group discussion sections, helping with grading and conferring frequently with the professor, who shouldered the burden of the instruction. Then, as now, the degree process took many years, but those who did earn their Ph.D. could look forward to a tenure-track job that, if all went well, would yield a secure, prestigious, decently paying position in an intellectually alive community. Only the campus radicals talked about unions for graduate students.

For some students who, like me, began their doctoral programs in the last decade, that apprenticeship model seems broken beyond repair. To us, the modern university resembles not a haven of mentoring and academic cooperation, but rather an efficiency-minded corporation that exploits our low-paid labor. We flocked into doctoral programs between the late '80s and the mid-'90s, partially because the conventional wisdom held that mass retirements of professors hired in the postwar era would mean many good jobs. Few of us, however, foresaw that universities would replace many tenure-track positions with part-time and adjunct positions, neither of which typically offers benefits, job security or, equally important, the protections of academic freedom. In 1970, according to the National Center for Education Statistics, 22 percent of the professoriate occupied part-time jobs. By 1997, that number was 42 percent.

Nor did we anticipate that as part of this restructuring of the educational work force—the casualization of academic work—big universities would also begin to rely on graduate teaching assistants as sources of cheap labor. At the University of Kansas, for example, the Kansas Public Employee Relations Board found that TAs in the English department had taught zero upper-level undergraduate courses in 1979, but 25 of them in 1993. The TAs' work that year cost the university "$51,297 as compared to $209,413 if faculty members had been hired," the board said. At many major universities, graduate students now handle as much as half of the entire teaching load.

As our classroom duties have increased, they have also changed character. The TAs' job description has "evolved over time," says Richard Hurd, a professor of labor studies at Cornell University. "They went from discussion group leaders and teachers of summer classes to essentially part-time faculty." Once we assisted professors by grading papers. Now we teach courses—sometimes even large lecture courses—on our own. The burden of teaching undergraduates is shifting from the tenured faculty to us. Little wonder that, as teaching undergraduates increasingly has become our responsibility, many of us identify ourselves not as "apprentices" but rather as campus employees who contribute significantly to the economic well-being of our institutions.

In addition, graduate student organizers across the country point to disproportionate wages paid per course (professors generally get far higher rates, sometimes for teaching the same courses), declining or nonexistent health benefits, rising tuition and enrollment fees, and the absence of effective grievance procedures. At Maryland, the university's own financial aid office states that graduate students need $12,375 to live adequately in the metropolitan area for nine months. Yet TAs in the English department there receive only about $9,800 per school year after taxes, according to student organizers.

Several organizers at GW described their grievances in an email to me: "The majority of part-time faculty and graduate teaching assistants at GWU are denied a living wage, health care coverage, child care, and realistic job descriptions. We are excluded from departmental meetings; we have no job security and work on a contingent semester-to-semester basis. We have no means to negotiate collectively for the terms of our employment. In addition, we are not provided adequate administrative support, and we work without the office space and other facilities needed to teach students well."

GW spokeswoman Barbara Porter replied in another e-mail that the university disputes some of those claims (though she declined to say which ones) and questions unionization's possible "impact on teaching and research." GW, she said, also maintains that "unionization would be inconsistent with the student status of our graduate teaching assistants."

Opponents of unions for graduate students often rest their case on this distinction. At Yale University, for example, where a high-profile TA-unionization campaign continues to generate acrimony on all sides, the administration insists that graduate students are first and foremost students, not employees. To qualify for protection under the National Labor Relations Act, graduate students must make the case that this is a distinction without a difference.

Yale Provost Alison Richard said last year, "We deeply believe that our graduate students are here primarily to be students." The university maintains that only 10 percent of its courses are led by graduate students. But when TA-led discussion sections are figured into the total number of hours of teaching a Yale undergraduate receives, it turns out that about 40 percent of those hours are the responsibility of TAs, according to a 1999 report issued by the Graduate Employees and Students Organization at the university. No understanding of the terms "student" or "apprentice" can accommodate the sober reality that, despite its huge endowment, Yale employs graduate students as teachers.

Many professors are concerned that the adversarial character of unionization could disrupt the mentoring relationship between graduate students and their faculty advisers, and possibly harm the teaching of undergraduates. Student-teacher relationships often require an unusual measure of trust, even a certain sort of intimacy.

Those concerns seem reasonable. Yet efficiency-minded administrators, not unions, have fostered the conditions for such anxiety. They have turned courses into commodities and made teachers, whether graduate students or professors, interchangeable. A 1999 survey conducted by a Tufts University professor on the issue of faculty-graduate student mentoring suggests that unions do not disrupt learning. The study asked 300 faculty members at five institutions that recognize TA unions whether collective bargaining had harmed mentoring. Ninety percent said it had not.

Do unions threaten undergraduate teaching? Little evidence suggests they do. In fact, graduate student organizers making their case almost always include among their demands better teacher-training programs and other teacher-support mechanisms for graduate students. Some unions may end up defining their interests narrowly, shirking broader teaching concerns, but nothing in the principle of unionization makes that outcome necessary.

In truth, TA unions likely will not alter the basic structure of graduate education. Their presence on campus signals the extent to which American universities have evolved into stratified economic enterprises. Organizers at Maryland, GW and elsewhere have allied with part-time and adjunct instructors partly as a practical strategy, but also as a way to demonstrate the common plight of all non-tenured knowledge workers. Some organizing drives have included non-academic staff, such as janitors, cooks, and house-cleaners. When these broad coalitions form around shared issues of disproportionate pay, unsteady work and inadequate health coverage, what does that say about universities? It says college teaching has been downgraded from a noble profession to another transaction in the service economy.

NOAM CHOMSKY
AND ACADEMIC HISTORY

N oam Chomsky has written more than 30 books over the last three decades. Yet neither the *Journal of American History*, nor the *American Historical Review*, nor *Reviews in American History* has reviewed them. If the journals had overlooked one or two of Chomsky's books, then the omissions might not rise to the status of a problem, and could be attributed to a combination of reasons, each of them incidental to Chomsky himself. If the journals had in fact devoted attention to him, but the preponderance of the attention had been hostile, then they might stand accused of harboring a bias. This is the most respectable way to disagree about such matters. But the journals have not done enough to deserve the accusation. They have not reviewed a single one of his books. Chomsky is one of most widely read political intellectuals in the world. Academic history pretends he does not exist. Why is this so?

A moment's reflection rules out the easiest explanations. No formal policy could have held up against multiple changes in the editorships of the journals. Even a tacit conspiracy is unthinkable given the upheavals of the last three decades. The journals have absorbed, presented, and guided an explosion of historical writing, and their formal commitment to intellectual pluralism has remained intact. As the editor of the *Journal of American History* wrote in 2004, "Through our book reviews, we aim to serve as the journal of record for American history."

Is Chomsky left out because he writes about topics of little interest to historians? His books contain arresting arguments about the history of the Cold War, genocide, terrorism, democracy, international affairs, nationalism, social policy, public opinion, health care, and militarism, and this merely begins the list. He ranges across the Americas, Europe, and Asia, paying special attention to the emergence of the United States. Two of his major themes, namely, the "rise of the West" in the context of comparative "global history," are also major areas of interest for professional historians, never more so than today.

Is Chomsky left out because he is not a professional historian? The journals have reviewed such non-historians as Robert Bellah, Randall Collins, Michel Foucault, Clifford Geertz, Nathan Glazer, Irving Howe, Seymour Martin Lipset, Richard Rorty, Edward Said, and John Updike because the books in question show a strong historical component. Chomsky, in any case, presents his evidence with an extensive record of citation, and keeps the rhetorical content of his writings extremely low.

Is Chomsky left out because he does not divorce his politics from his history? Academic historians often use their skills as instruments of political abuse and intimidation, as Sean Wilentz did in his testimony before Congress a few years ago, or as David Landes did in a letter to the *New York Times* in 2000, in which he wrote, "If Mr. Nader thinks people will forget that he has been willing to bring grave harm to his country, he is in for a big surprise." If this sort of thing made acceptable grounds for exclusion from the community of scholars, few historians would have learned to honor Arthur Schlesinger, Jr., who is, manifestly, a liberal historian. A profession that made the divorce of politics and history a condition of entry would have packed away Schlesinger, Landes, and Wilentz in disgrace a long time ago. Professional history does not (and should not) do anything of the kind. The same point holds with only slightly less force in the case of Henry Kissinger. *Reviews in American History*, having passed up all opportunities to review Chomsky's books, described Kissinger's *Diplomacy* (1994) as "a masterful, brilliant, and provocative account of world politics and American foreign policy from Cardinal Richelieu to the end of the Cold War."

Schlesinger's liberalism mirrors the dominant ideological gestures in history writing. But to stop here would be to dump the whole question into the realm of biases. It would be to employ a loose sociology of knowledge to argue that the journals serve some ideologies to the exclusion of other ideologies. The trouble with this explanation is that the journals in fact have become open to ideas that claim to have surpassed liberalism: postcolonalism, poststructuralism, and so on. More to the point, they have not been shy in throwing open their pages to Marxism. Why Eric Hobsbawm, but not Noam Chomsky?

I suspect the answer lies less with Chomsky's arguments, and still less with his professional status, than with his intentions. The history of liberalism and Marxism in the academy has been the history of a science of concepts. The main responsibility of the liberal or Marxist intellectual, accordingly, has been to discover new material, which involves correcting and re-correcting biases in past scholarship, a sort of intellectual forensics. The science of concepts not only parallels the development of institutions; it requires their continual enlargement and aggrandizement.

Chomsky's anarchist interpretation of responsibility points elsewhere. "It is the responsibility of intellectuals to speak the truth and to expose lies." One cannot read Chomksy's books and easily conclude that truth is something to be surrounded by a gang of concepts, or driven into specialized routines or "think tanks" (a phrase which ought to discredit itself in the presence of a mind awake.) He does not say, with the post-liberal historians, that academic intellectuals need a whole new vocabulary to understand social reality. He does not think of historical writing as a pathway to power, tenure, faculty club dinners, fund-raising, or anything else of this sort. His anarchism teaches him to view social status as a form of domination.

This explanation is crude, but it suggests how the current generation of professional historians, many of them beginning in the restless mood of the 1960s and 1970s, have fitted themselves so effortlessly into the hierarchical arrangements of academic life. They have liberalized it to include once-marginalized social groups, but have done very little to reverse the repression of labor power. Today, the difference between a free professional and a university employee has been virtually erased. History's professional societies preside over a structure of domination far greater in its scope and power than at any time in the past.

Whatever the cause, the consequences have impoverished us all. The isolation forces Chomsky to meet tests of personality few contemporary figures are asked to meet. Everything from the tone of his writings to the recesses of his biography come up for harsh review. His critic finds a factual error and meets it with a cry of "Aha!" Or, if no factual errors are at hand, the critic cries, "Too simple." Instead of engaging in research and discussion that might give the argument more nuance or variety, the critic stops reading. Accreditation, not argument, likewise dominates the reaction of the followers. Attracted to Chomsky for his isolation, they impute to him quasi-magical qualities. A glance at his published interviews will indicate how frequently he attempts to discourage his cult-like following.

The journals, by excluding one of the most influential voices in contemporary political discussion, betray a selective commitment to intellectual freedom. One of the lessons we have learned from post-liberal ideas is that censorship involves subtle relationships between culture and social processes. Silence may be produced and sustained as easily as argument.

The profession's recovery of principle is not the only reason for putting a halt to its exclusion of Chomsky. Many of the articles and reviews in the journals lack connections to human responsibilities. They meet the demand for relevance without posing the question: relevant to what?

It is the misfortune of liberal and Marxist historians to be writing in the age of conservative ascendancy. For decades they have managed the ideological interests of parties close to power, only to discover, belatedly, that their metaphysics of progress have betrayed them. They grind their concepts into finer and finer points, narrow inquiry into specialties and sub-specialities. In forsaking the fields of intelligence for the technologies of reason, however, they produce an effluvia of permanent surrender. Probably so many young people find Chomsky bracing and invigorating because so much of our scholarly culture is passionless.

The point is not that Chomsky is free of faults, or that he is correct in his interpretations, or that my explanations are adequate to the problem posed. The burden here is to articulate a warrant for his inclusion in the pages of the leading journals in history. Perhaps a forum on "Chomsky and the History of American Foreign Policy" would spur mutual enlightenment. Who could fail to learn something from a debate between Noam Chomsky and John Lewis Gaddis?

THE END OF SOCIOLOGY?

A bout a decade ago university administrators began closing sociology departments and reducing funding for the survivors. For a brief time sociology seemed to face wholesale elimination. A rash of eulogies appeared in the journals, followed by recriminations, and before long the field degenerated into the kind of academic narcissism that accompanies plummeting prestige. In this way, the end-of-sociology literature supplied evidence for the main allegation against the field, that it had retreated into parochialism.

In a reply to these developments, *Whose Keeper? Social Science and Moral Obligation* (1989), Alan Wolfe traced the ironic emergence of a "sociology without society." Rather than endlessly elaborating theories of state and economy, he said, professional sociologists could recover their vitality by helping citizens understand the moral conflicts generated by these institutions. Civil society served as the natural location for sociological inquiry. *An Intellectual in Public*, Wolfe's essays, provides a splendid example of the sort of civic work sociologists might pursue. The collection consists of work first published in magazines such as the *New Republic*, the *Atlantic Monthly*, and the *Chronicle of Higher Education*. Read straight through, it advances two propositions.

First, it suggests the book review as a vehicle for popular education. For many years newspapers and magazines have offered themselves as such agents of public awareness. In practice, their review sections often collapse under the weight of political, financial, and status pressures that accompany the publication of new books. Wolfe resists these pressures as effectively as any critic now writing. His essay "Anti-American Studies" excoriates recent developments in the academic field of American studies, charging its leftist leaders with a hatred of their subject. Wolfe also eviscerates conservatives in their institutional home: the policy institute. In "The Revolution That Never Was" he explains why "conservatives in America have been unable to come up with any sustained and significant ideas capable of giving substance to their complaints against the modern world. I say ideas, not slogans." That Wolfe's book instructs so judiciously and skillfully in the leading issues of our time, much more so than the sociology journals, seems to me a genuine achievement. Wolfe says he began writing reviews out of curiosity and only later came to understand the task as a contribution to democracy. *An Intellectual in Public* gives every reason to believe him.

But the collection's second proposition miscarries. The main fault of our books, according to Wolfe, lies with their dependence on ideology. He never says what he means by "ideology." Sometimes it signifies a set of ideas wrapped too tightly around an author's political views. Other times, Wolfe makes ideology take the blame for sloppy research. The proposition becomes a shibboleth. Wolfe believes that Americans hate politics, desire consensus, and observe moderate taste and opinion. If we have learned anything from the neo-liberalism of the 1990s, it is that such a complex of beliefs raises an ideology all its own, replete with hidden political imperatives. In any case, the soft form of ideology provides some discipline to thought. Given the omnipresence of slogans, scandals, and images in our public life, maybe we need more ideology, not less.

We surely need to improve our collective imagination. This idea guides Steven P. Dandaneau's *Taking It Big: Developing Sociological Consciousness in Postmodern Times*, another book that tries to inject a note of vitality into academic sociology by finding a public purpose for it. Dandaneau, professor of sociology at the University of Dayton, has none of Wolfe's suspicion of reform. Thinking sociologically, Dandaneau says, entails a radical form of awareness, an imagination capable of reflecting on experience by grasping connections between self and world. This heightened awareness throws up dilemmas the solving of which becomes its main task. What is the role of individual action in environmental degradation? What is the role of environmental degradation in the health of individuals? "This book is, therefore, ultimately about politics."

Like Peter Berger's *Invitation to Sociology*, for many years the best brief introduction to the field, *Taking It Big* argues that the sociological perspective is, by definition, a critical form of consciousness. That something lurks behind reality is axiomatic to social reflection. Received political truths get no exemption. Dandaneau accordingly has many sharp words for contemporary society. On the other hand, when he discusses disabled children, Generation X, and contemporary religion—themes on which the book pivots—he betrays no prefabricated "ideology." Judged against the crop of new books trying to make sociology compelling to students, *Taking It Big* is especially inviting, even charming. How many books take the time to instruct in the proper pronunciation of Max Weber (Vey-ber)?

∎∎∎

In spite of the disappointment that carries the mood of these books, Wolfe and Dandaneau conclude with a feeling of qualified hope about the future of social study. Why? In part, it's because they are sensitive, as most of their peers are not, to a tradition of non-specialized sociology that has persisted alongside the professional ethos they deplore. Unlike the radical sociologists of the 1960s, who faced a comparable crisis, Dandaneau and Wolfe do not call for a "New Sociology." Instead, they see the task as one of renewal.

Even this more modest aspiration meets overwhelming obstacles. In the first place, persuading sociologists to pay attention to alternative traditions means confronting the methodological fetishism and scientific pretension that have dominated the field for a half-century. It implies, moreover, a challenge to the very organization of academic life. Professional specialities have so completely fragmented our collective cultural resources that academic intellectuals of each new generation must struggle against their chosen field if they hope, with Wolfe and Dandaneau, to apply their ideas to public problems. This struggle has its own history, but now it may present the most severe challenge.

Nonetheless, the tradition by which public intellectuals hope to resurrect sociology asks compelling questions. What is the American character? No professional sociologist yet has answered this question with as much verve and ingenuity as Alexis de Tocqueville in *Democracy in America*, which repays rereading. Tocqueville believed the rise of equality enacted one of the great dramas in the history of humankind. "This whole book has been written under the impulse of a kind of religious dread inspired by contemplation of this irresistible revolution advancing century by century over every obstacle and even now going forward amid the ruins it has itself created."

Equality, Tocqueville said, worked paradoxical effects on American character. For example, equality overturned the languid psychology of fixed classes common to aristocracies, and sent a superabundance of energy coursing through democratic social life. Lacking a stable foundation for their opinions, Americans gained a keen feeling for the power of individual reason to win the world. This confidence in turn generated an astonishing level of experimentation and innovation. At the same time, equality granted that virtue was equally distributed throughout society, and this predisposed each individual to surrender moral and intellectual authority to the majority. Public opinion, rooted in the power of individual reason, continually poisoned its source. Tocqueville concluded that public opinion imposed itself "on men's very souls." The American character was simultaneously the most innovative and the most conservative in the world.

Tocqueville called for a new class of intellectuals to educate the populace in such ironies. He could not have anticipated that irony would accompany even this cry. As the social studies developed in the United States on the model of natural science, they proved less and less able to recognize the sort of broad inquiry Tocqueville practiced. Had *Democracy in America* appeared in the 1950s it might have been dismissed by sociologists as the work of a talented amateur.

This was nearly the fate of the decade's most brilliant inquiry into the national character, *The Lonely Crowd*.

David Riesman, its chief author, did not have a doctorate in sociology. He took a law degree at Harvard, then worked as assistant to the treasurer at the Sperry Gyroscope Company in New York. The interviews that form the heart of the book bucked a trend within sociology to standardize and quantify the relationship between investigator and interviewee. Riesman treated the interviews as an aspect of the art of conversation. For these reasons sociologists treated the book coolly, at least until a reading public made it a bestseller and put Riesman on the cover of *Time*. *The Lonely Crowd* went on to sell more than 1.4 million copies.

The book's inquiry into "the Changing American Character," as the subtitle read, addressed a generation demoralized by war, over-organized by bureaucracy, and over-socialized by the routines of family and friendship. Riesman noticed that older forms of character were rapidly disappearing in the face of these developments. Neither the "tradition-directed" nor the "inner-directed" type, he argued, could long withstand the centripetal forces set in motion by the corporate economy, which encouraged a new, "other-directed" type.

The inner-directed American followed an internal "Gyroscope," immune to external pressure. The tradition-directed American obeyed archaic customs and rules. The new American, by contrast, was more malleable, more passive. Other-direction came to signify mindless conformity, although Riesman's insights into the connections between conduct, inner life, and social organization bore a more complicated analysis. The distinction of the book lay in a paradox worthy of Tocqueville. In the midst of their abundance, middle-class Americans felt weak, isolated, as anxious as ever.

Successors to *Democracy in America* and *The Lonely Crowd*, books such as Christopher Lasch's *The Culture of Narcissism* (1979) and Robert Bellah's *Habits of the Heart* (1985) share an attempt to grasp the traits of the American character. At its best this attempt can make only partial, time-bound judgments. These books commend themselves to us today because they solicit our attention as members of the commonwealth. What sort of people are Americans? No question could be more romantic to a "sociology without society." In these days of confusion and distress, however, no question could be more urgent.

II

■■■

HISTORY AS CRITICISM

■■■

JAMES AGEE,
THE ANARCHIST SUBLIME

I n recent years American publishers have released collections of
essays by Alfred Kazin and Lionel Trilling, letters by Robert
Lowell, Dwight Macdonald, and C. Wright Mills, and biographies of John Kenneth Galbraith, Richard Hofstadter, Irving Howe,
Edmund Wilson, and Richard Yates. For scholars and writers coming-
of-age, the quickening of interest in these mid-century intellectuals
means a chance to remember the lives of our grandfathers, before
personal computers, before the status revolution in higher education,
before television and its drizzle of images.

James Agee is the latest figure to solicit our attention, now that
the Library of America has dedicated a pair of volumes to his career
as a journalist, poet, critic, essayist, novelist, and screenwriter. The
volumes join a revival in progress. In 2005, a James Agee Celebration was held in Knoxville, his home town; a book appeared about
his friendship with Charlie Chaplin; and Fordham University Press
reprinted his long essay on Brooklyn. *Agee Agonistes*, a collection of
scholarly essays, appeared in 2007 from the University of Tennessee
Press, which is planning *The Works of James Agee* in nine volumes.

These projects should put the lie to the complaint, circulating
since Agee's premature death in 1955, that he wasted his talent in
drink and depression. Once the range of his achievement comes
fully into view, it may be that the variety of his writing explains his
reputation as an underachiever. Then again, to envision Agee as a
success subtracts from his sensibility. Tall and gangly, he walked in
graceless strides, arms and hands flailing. Photographs that show
him in a frayed blazer might commend him to today's middle-class

writer, although, in truth, his manners and attitudes shared more with Chaplin's Tramp, whom he idolized. They disliked the same three kinds of people: the rich, the genteel, and the police.

Agee died at forty-five, indebted and uninsured. *Let Us Now Praise Famous Men*, his masterpiece, was out of print, along with the rest of his major writings. *A Death in the Family*, his novel, was incomplete and unpublished. This record of failure, so noticeable to his critics, has hidden away the coherence of his literary biography. Agee courted failure deliberately, until it grew into a method. He thought of himself as an anarchist, living in and through a special sensibility. The preamble to *Let Us Now Praise Famous Men* set forth its first premise. "Every fury on earth has been absorbed in time, as art, or as religion, or as authority in one form or another. The deadliest blow the enemy of the human soul can strike is to do fury honor. Swift, Blake, Beethoven, Christ, Joyce, Kafka, name me a one who has not been thus castrated. Official acceptance is the one unmistakable symptom that salvation is beaten again."

Agee's fury began on May 18, 1916, the day his father was killed in an automobile accident. He was six years old at the time, and little in his later life suggests that he recovered from the loss. Between ages ten and fourteen, he lived at St. Andrews, an Episcopal school near Sewanee, Tennessee. *The Morning Watch*, a novella he composed about this period, took fatherlessness as its leitmotif, once in lamentation for Agee's missing father, once again in yearning for a spiritual surrogate. Orphaned male writers often want to test the limits of their talent against contrived obstacles. Agee's fury, though, did not inflame in him a will to power, nor did it nurture in him a sense of victimhood. Of sidelong flashes of anger at his mother, there were many. She had him circumcised at age eight, and, after enrolling him in St. Andrews, she hid her diffidence behind her piety. "Mumsy you were so genteel/ That you made your son a heel. /Sunnybunch must now reclaim/ From the sewerpipe of his shame/ Any little coin he can/ To reassure him he's a man."

After leaving St. Andrews, Agee spent one year in Knoxville High School, then went north to Philips Exeter Academy, and afterward, Harvard. Upon graduation in 1932, he went directly from Cambridge to New York to take a staff position at *Fortune*.

Most writers encompass a wider range of personal experience. At sixteen, Agee traveled to England and France for a bicycle trip with Father Flye, his St. Andrews teacher and mentor. He never returned to Europe. In New York, he associated with actors and writers with temperaments and backgrounds similar to his. He described his work for the Luce publications as a "semisuicide," but he did not quit until 1948, when he moved to California to write screenplays for John Huston. Soon after he relocated, he suffered a heart attack that foreshortened his collaboration with Huston and ruined his own desire to direct.

"I am essentially an anarchist," Agee wrote in 1938. He professed his allegiance on numerous occasions and never contradicted himself. In an autobiographical statement in 1942, he referred to himself as an "armchair anarchist." Two years later, in a profile for *Life* magazine, he portrayed Huston as "a natural-born antiauthoritarian individualistic libertarian anarchist, without portfolio." The following year, Agee again allied himself with "the sentiments and ideas of something practically extinct—the old-fashioned, nonviolent anarchist." This figure he imagined to have been "a warm, generous-hearted, compassionate, angry man who really *did* love freedom." All these remarks have been published since 1962. Biographers and critics have made nothing of them. Reviewers of the Library of America volumes evaded the subject entirely. Why the silence?

Ignorance, for one thing. As Dwight Macdonald once pointed out, "Anarchism does not mean 'chaos' as the *New York Times* and most American editorialists think. It just means 'without a leader.'" Anarchism cultivates political practices independent of the modern power-state and its corporate allies. Rather than vanguardism, it encourages direct, democratic participation. Rather than the formation of establishments, it encourages voluntary associations vitalized by spontaneous effusions and organized around the latent potentialities of cooperation.

Agee did not join any political party, and voted just once. In holding himself aloof from the factionalism of the mid-century years, he honored his naturally generous temperament. During Charlie Chaplin's last, raucous press conference in New York, it was Agee, speaking from the rafters, who challenged the anticommunist newspapermen. Then again, his friend Whittaker Chambers showed up late one night at his Greenwich Village apartment, drunk and distraught, and fell asleep on his couch sobbing about the communists.

What little Agee had to say about real politics is enough to make one glad he did not say more. He characterized World War II as "a rattlesnake-skunk choice, with the skunk of course considerably less deadly yet not so desirable around the house that I could back him with any favor." He wrote a bitter satire on the bombing of Hiroshima, followed by an apocalyptic screenplay for Chaplin on the subject of thermonuclear holocaust. It was possible to support the war and condemn the bomb, and the stance could arise from mutually supporting moral and political convictions. In 1943, Agee recorded his pessimism for the coming postwar order: "I expect the worst of us and of the English; something so little better in most respects (if we get our way) than Hitler would bring, that the death of a single man is a disgrace between the two."

If the political content of anarchism exhausted its significance, then it might merit nothing more than a footnote in Agee's biography. But this is not so. More than an attitude, less than a creed, anarchism was to Agee a loosely worn skirt to defend the creativity of perception against the metaphysics of the concept and its embodiment in the specialist system, by which experience was isolated, desiccated, and vitiated. As he wrote in 1950, "Allegiance to 'the modern mind' must have deprived countless intellectuals of most of their being. Certainly among many I have known or read, feeling and intuition are suspect, sensation is isolated, only the thinking faculty is thoroughly respected;

the chances of interplay among these faculties, and of mutual discipline and fertilization, are reduced to a minimum."

A constellation of American writers articulated surprisingly similar sentiments after the 1930s and before the 1960s, surprising because their history remains to be written. The leading narrative follows the journey of the mid-century avant-garde from Marxism to neo-conservatism and registers the prepossessing influence of European literature and philosophy. But there is another story, a return *from* European metaphysics *to* the indigenous temper of anarchism.

This story is laid away in letters, diaries, interviews, and biographies. Edward Abbey rebelled against his father's Marxism and tried to write "A General Theory of Anarchism" throughout the 1950s before settling on "Anarchism and the Morality of Violence" for his master's thesis in philosophy, filed at the University of New Mexico in 1959. Dwight Macdonald resigned his Marxism in the 1940s and began calling himself a "conservative anarchist." Paul Goodman introduced himself as "an old-fashioned anarchist" while C. Wright Mills wrote, a few months after publishing *The Power Elite* in 1956, "What these jokers—all of them—don't realize is that way down deep and systematically I'm a goddamn anarchist."

Robert Lowell, writing to Flannery O'Connor in 1954, noted that "Henry Adams called himself a conservative, Catholic anarchist; I would take this for myself, only adding agnostic." Lowell, like Agee, was packed off to an Episcopal boarding school as a youth. He, too, found himself in the grip of the "idealistic unreal morality and the insipid blackness of the Episcopalian church."

Here lies a clue to the ethical value of anarchism. "I feel bound to be an anarchist in religion as well as 'politics,'" Agee wrote in 1938, contending that "the effort toward good in both is identical, and that a man who wants and intends good cannot afford to have the slightest respect for that which is willing to accept it as it is, or to be pleased with a 'successful' compromise."

Agee discovered the "effort toward good" from Father James Harold Flye, who joined the history faculty at St. Andrews one year before he arrived and served as his moral tutor thereafter. The inheritance weighed heavily on him. At Phillips Exeter, where his desire to write awakened, then again at Harvard, he offered public displays of his piety. In 1934, when his first book of poems was published, the volume seemed to his friend Robert Fitzgerald "the work of a desperate Christian." Even after his despair lifted and his belief scattered, his voice retained a religious penumbra. In 1950, he participated in a *Partisan Review* symposium: "Religion and the Intellectuals." How, he asked in his contribution, could secular intellectuals mock the idea of transubstantiation while they accredited the idea of penis envy? "It is fashionable to feel," he continued in this spirit, "and to force upon others, an acute sense of social responsibility; but it is rare to find a non-religious person who recognizes what is meant by sinning against oneself, or who recognizes that, granting extenuating circumstances, every person is crucially responsible for his thoughts and actions."

Solicitude for Father Flye coincided with Agee's scorn for churches, vestments, and hierocracies. The Reverend Harry Powell, the murdering preacher in *The Night of the Hunter* (1955—Agee co-wrote the screenplay) bears the sublimated terror of his devotionals at St. Andrews. The script for Chaplin, *The Tramp's New World*, abounds in anticlerical attitudes. Then there is Father Jackson in *A Death in the Family*, Agee's novel about the automobile crash that killed his father. Two-thirds of the way through, he juxtaposes a remarkable pair of scenes. In the first, Mary, alone in her room after news of her husband's accident reaches her, pleads with her God to tell her why this horrible event has befallen her. In the next scene, Rufus encounters a crew of older boys from the neighborhood. They ask him to dance for their pleasure. Suspicious that they are tricking him, yet desperate to win their approval, his moral perplexity mirrors his mother's. The juxtaposition poses the problem of theodicy, the traditional jurisdiction of priests and theologians, but Agee refused to allow Father Jackson an uncontradicted answer. "I tell you Rufus, it's enough to make a man puke up his soul," says Mary's brother, Andrew, at the end of the novel. "That—that butterfly has got more of God in him than Jackson will ever see for the rest of eternity. Prig-gish, meanly-mouthed son of a bitch."

The Night of the Hunter and *A Death in the Family* use the undivided intuitions of children to point out that ecclesiastical guardianship over morality rests on false riddles and trumped-up antagonisms. The film, written from the perspective of two children, shows the Reverend Powell (played by Robert Mitchum) with "Love" tattooed on the knuckles of one hand, and "Hate" on the other. In the novel, the last word is given to Rufus (the young Agee) as he puzzles over his Uncle Andrew's outburst. Andrew had directed the outburst toward the family as well as Father Jackson. Rufus wonders why:

"He hates them just like opening a furnace door but he doesn't want them to know it. He doesn't want them to know it because he doesn't want to hurt their feelings. He doesn't want them to know it because he knows they love him and think he loves them. He doesn't want them to know it because he loves them. But how can he love them if he hates them so? How can he hate them if he loves them? Is he mad at them because they can say their prayers and he doesn't? He could if he wanted to, why doesn't he? Because he hates prayers. And them too for saying them. He wished he could ask his uncle, 'Why do you hate Mama?' but he was afraid to."

The ethical dimension of Agee's anarchism entails the same double-sided consequences as his anti-politics. He cast off the super-intending influence of religious dogma, and rejected its metaphysics of good and evil, on the assumption that "every person is crucially responsible for his thoughts and actions." The liability of this utopian attitude toward personal responsibility was tumult omnipresent, a ceaseless struggle against the poison of ambivalence. An emotional life divested of the metaphysical confidence of religious morality stands undefended before passion's caprice, as Agee demonstrated in deciding to write a love letter to his ex-wife, Alma.

He decided to write to Alma (as he explained in the letter) after Helen Levitt showed him a photograph she had taken of them when they were married, "and seeing it, fourteen years dropped out from under me, and I knew just where we were then, and where we really belong, and where we always ought to be. I am still in love with you, Alma" The background is important. Alma Mailman had fallen for Agee when he was still married to her friend Olivia Saunders, the favorite daughter of a prominent New York family. To punish Alma for the affair, the Saunders family shunned her. In her own family, only her father did not break ties. Marrying Agee washed away part of the stain. Then disaster struck. Less than one month after Alma gave birth to their child, Agee confessed that he had been sleeping with Mia Fritsch, a researcher at *Fortune*. Alma boarded a freighter to Mexico.

When he wrote the letter beckoning Alma to return, he was forty-three. He had a third wife (Mia) and two children under his care. Alma, forty years old, had remarried as well, also with two children. The letter proposed, in effect, that they do it all over again, that they smash up two families and begin anew. All because he got a glimpse of an old photograph.

An autobiographical statement confessed the vulnerability behind the immorality: "he is pronouncedly schizoid and a manic-depressive as well, with an occasional twinkle of paranoia." Others saw Agee as he saw himself: the children who chalked on the steps of his home in Brooklyn, "The Man Who Lives Here is a Loony"; and Thomas Wolfe, who reported, after a long evening of conversation, that Agee was "crazy," that he "was always talking about things in spirals and on planes and things." A colleague at *Time*, overhearing a drunken Agee cursing a telephone operator, was moved to say that "a wild yearning violence beat in his blood, certainly, as just as certainly, the steadier pulse of a saint."

Lionel Trilling found the necessary distinctions. During the last conversation he had with Agee, they talked about the concept of ambivalence in Freud's *The Ego and the Id*: loving and hating at the same time. Agee said it disgusted him. "It seemed to me then," Trilling wrote, "that his brilliant intensities of perception and his superb rhetoric required him to affirm, if not actually to believe, that the human soul could exist in a state of radical innocence which was untouched by any contrary."

▮▮▮

Let Us Now Praise Famous Men bore James Agee's most conspicuous traits: his oscillating voice, perpetually prepared for paralysis; his dislike of ordinary politics; his determination to cut his perceptions down to the bone of innocence; his struggle to find a place to stand in a ruined world.

The background is well known. In 1936, *Fortune* sent Agee and the photographer Walker Evans to Alabama. They were to file a report on conditions in tenant farming. Agee and Evans lived briefly with three impoverished families. The following year, Agee rented a house with Alma in Frenchtown, New Jersey, and set to work. He wrote in pencil, at night, breaking his concentration to read passages aloud to Alma and to confer with Evans and Dwight Macdonald, Robert Fitzgerald, and Delmore Schwartz. It was in Frenchtown in 1938 that he wrote the letter to Father Flye in which he first called himself an anarchist.

Concern for the plight of Southern farmers had not been so active since the 1890s. Twenty-seven years old, Agee was running strong in his talent. Yet he squandered his chance to make himself heard. The book added little, if anything, to the general stock of ideas about tenant farming. Long patches of the prose were opaque. *Fortune* rejected the initial essay; the publisher deferred the book after arguing with the authors. By the time it appeared, in 1941, the war held a monopoly of national concern. *Let Us Now Praise Famous Men* sold about six hundred copies in its first year, a few thousand more in remainder, and quietly went out of print. Trilling said he rarely heard anybody mention it in the 1940s and 1950s, not even in private conversation.

Agee went out of his way to fend off the sympathies of his readers. In the preamble he copied out the famous final sentences of *The Communist Manifesto*, but then added, in a note to "the average reader," that "these words are quoted here to mislead those who will be misled by them." In fact, "neither these words nor the authors are the property of any political party, faith, or faction." Agee knew enough about politics to understand the economic and social forces buffeting the lives of the sharecroppers. He understood, as they could not, the real calamity of their situation. Yet he rejected the meliorism of the liberal reformers as firmly as he rejected the radicalism of the communists: "This particular subject of tenantry is becoming more and more stylish as a focus of 'reform,' and in view of the people who will suffer and be betrayed at the hands of such 'reformers,' there could never be enough effort to pry their eyes open even a little wider."

The surrealist movement made its way from Paris to New York in the 1930s. A decade later, the New Fiction matured in the United States, spurred by translations of Kafka and Kierkegaard. *Let Us Now Praise Famous Men* could have been taken up as an example of experimental writing, if Agee had not choked off an aesthetic interpretation as well. "It is funny if I am a surrealist," he wrote in his journal in January 1938. This moment of bemusement soured in the book's preamble. "Above all else: in God's name don't think of it as Art," he admonished.

There remained the possibility that Agee would appeal to the conscience of his readers. But the preamble resembled the opening pages of *Old Goriot*, in which Balzac bemoaned the bourgeois turn toward spectatorship in the presence of human pain. "Their hearts are momentarily touched," Balzac wrote, "but the impression made on them is fleeting, it vanishes as quickly as a delicious fruit melts in the mouth." Agee likewise supposed that his "average reader" would be edified, nothing more, by his portraits of suffering. Scorning "your safe world," he borrowed the title of his book from *Ecclesiasticus*. The irony came at the expense of his readers.

The failing of the book was the main condition of its achievement. Agee intended it as "an effort in human actuality." Only by antagonizing ready-made techniques of observation did he believe that he could hope to respect, understand, contemplate, and love the sharecroppers as human beings. These were the positive dimensions of his mistrust of inherited forms of cultural authority. He went to Alabama to tell what it was like to be in the presence of a group of undefended, unfamiliar people located on the margins of society.

Rather than delineating a problem or an issue, rather than shading his observations into a logic of narrative, he wove a mosaic of braided perceptions, luminous and radiant. In describing a bed, or a pair of trousers, he illuminated the image as if he was bringing it forth for the first time as it had existed always.

To grasp the complexity of this aspiration, consider the conventions dishonored in the execution. Agee did not try to discover new knowledge about his subjects, like a social scientist. He did not present himself as spokesman, overflowing with humanitarian concern, or as a psychologist, building up case histories, or as an ideologist, advancing a science of concepts, or as an artist, falsifying reality in order to reenter selected aspects, or as a professional writer, extracting from his subject a set of techniques to be submitted for juridical or commercial status. These refusals, and the integrity and responsibility upon which they rested, released a flow of emotional and imaginative energy that transcended the impersonal networks of communication dominating Serious Literature in the United States. Few writers anywhere have applied a greater intensity or sophistication to the involutions of thought and feeling disarmed. Few have been so overwhelmed in the task. *Let Us Now Praise Famous Men* never found an encompassing vision. Agee presented his struggle to see with a grace and fury all his own.

▌▌▌

To forge a Concept out of this impulse to fail would rob anarchism of its essential qualities. For a long time now, the human sciences and their philosophical allies have emphasized the sovereignty of language over experience, have made thought and feeling intelligible as the interplay of text and context. But language may meet an impulse it reflects or constructs only by injuring. *Silence* dissolves when words bespeak it. *Privacy* scrutinized in public is no longer privacy. The meaning of *dreaming* lies in the forgetting. No genuine history of dreaming is possible, for its remembered experience, its forms, interpretations, and stigmata, constitute a loss of its reality.

So it is with anarchism, whose first principle acknowledges no first principles and whose success depends on consciousness of its inadequacies. It entails a receding horizon, a failing struggle against the trappings of institutions and ideologies. Not demonstration, explanation, and justification, but illumination lies at its center of its aspiration. Absurdity has been its recurring conclusion; satire its method, not merely for criticizing but profaning authority. The "zoological types" exemplified in Balzac's *Human Comedy* have shaped many of its impressions and images.

Typically, anarchist poets and writers do not agree on the name of its special source of energy. Agee named it "being" and "fury." E.E. Cummings named it "Is." Laura Riding named it "individual-unreal" and warned, in *Anarchism is Not Enough*, not to dilute it by analogy. That anarchism's source is hived in a preconscious region of the psyche, undiscoverable by language and hence ungovernable by reflective intelligence; on this essential point, they seem to agree.

Standing for the limits of *knowing* in an Age of Information, anarchism reports itself in maxims, epigrams, and aphorisms, by way of pamphlets and manifestos, when it reports itself at all. ("If I weren't an anarchist I would probably be a left-wing conservative," Agee wrote to Father Flye, "though I write even the words with superstitious dread.") Provocative and enigmatic, exiled and omnipresent, it is the tramp in the ghetto of mass culture.

Anarchism hides in history, while its rivals swim in sympathy with the times. The origins of the modern ideologies lie in a counter-intuitive discovery: man-made institutions may acquire an independent logic, which may turn to confront its makers. In *The Wealth of Nations*, Adam Smith put this discovery to work for liberalism, much as Karl Marx, in *Capital*, made communism answer "a social process that goes on behind the backs of the producers." Smith's mystical appeal to an "invisible hand," like Marx's attempt to master the "anarchy of production," whipped history and human nature into a logic of relations. As liberalism and Marxism developed, their ideological vanguards transformed the logic of relations into the science of concepts, built institutions to anchor the Enlightenment, and thereby reproduced themselves in the Association, Bureau, Center, Department, Institute, Office, Party, and University. Therein the intellectuals accumulate conceptual knowledge, score points against the adversary, diagnose crises, uncover scandals, and chronicle their own changing role in the Progress of History.

Agee wrote often about the power of film and photography to transcend inherited vocabularies of representation. But he reported his fidelity to anarchism fitfully, in fragments and outlines which may give the impression that it is chaotic, or merely eccentric. One such fragment, "Now as Awareness," ruminated on the necessity of "valuing life above art." The preamble to *Let Us Now Praise Famous Men*, setting the furies of creativity against the authority of art, religion, history, and society, bore a silent debt to Rousseau, whose "Discourse on the Sciences and the Arts" (1750) voiced the same idea in very nearly the same words: "Our souls have been corrupted in proportion as our sciences and our arts have advanced toward perfection." William Blake, another of the "unpaid agitators" accompanying Agee to Alabama, echoed the idea in *The Marriage of Heaven and Hell*: "The tygers of wrath are wiser than the horses of instruction."

Anarchism, so understood, substitutes for the process theory of history the ancient aphorism, "History is philosophy by example." It entrusts itself to a genealogy of spiritual striving. Not invisible processes, but feats of virtuosity renew it. Not a vanguard of intellectuals, but the annals of biography transmit it between the lines of history. Not ideology, but filiopiety. "Those works which I most deeply respect have about them a firm quality of the superhuman," Agee wrote, "in part because they refuse to define and limit and crutch, or admit themselves as human."

Marxists and liberals apply ideological and political tests to police their communities. Anarchists enjoin themselves as isolated stars in a common constellation. Of Jesus Christ, William Blake, Jonathan Swift, James Joyce, Franz Kafka, and Ludwig von Beethoven, Agee said "Some you 'study' and learn from; some corroborate you; some 'stimulate' you; some are gods; some are brothers, much closer than colleagues or gods; some choke the heart out of you and make you dubious of ever reading or looking at work again: but in general, you know yourself to be at least by knowledge and feeling, of and among these, a member in a race which is much superior to any organization or Group or Movement or Affiliation, and the bloody enemy of all such, no matter what their 'sincerity,' 'honesty,' or 'good intentions'." By such examples and encounters, he laid up ethical and aesthetic equivalents to the anarchist's characteristic political gesture in the "propaganda of the deed."

▌▌▌

The critical and commercial failure of *Let Us Now Praise Famous Men* Agee accepted without protest. No missives to his publisher; no carping about the critics who misunderstood his meaning; no bitterness toward the public who ignored his book. To his failing health he applied another kind of diffidence. In the spring of 1955, he was enduring five or six minor heart attacks every day, swallowing nitroglycerine tablets one after another. On May 11, he mailed his last letter to Father Flye: "Nothing much to report. I feel, in general, as if I were dying: a terrible slowing-down, in all ways, above all in relation to work." Five days later he died in a taxicab on his way to the doctor's office.

Agee's success began soon afterward. *A Death in the Family* won a Pulitzer Prize in 1958. Two years later, *Let Us Now Praise Famous Men* was republished to universal acclaim. Film critics, civil rights activists, and bohemian poets avidly read *Agee on Film* (1958), *Letters of James Agee to Father Flye* (1962), *The Collected Short Prose of James Agee* (1968), *The Collected Poems of James Agee* (1968), and *Remembering James Agee* (1974). The introduction to the republication of *The Morning Watch* compared him to Shelley. He became a legend, a cultural hero for a generation in love with cultural heroes.

All along Agee's distinction rested with a fraternity of sympathetic writers, "members," he might have agreed, "of a race which is much superior any organization or Group or Movement." C. Wright Mills praised *Let Us Now Praise Famous Men* for "the enormity of the self-chosen task" and dubbed it "sociological poetry." Paul Goodman thought "many of the items are presented with extraordinary beauty and power and a kind of isolated truth" and lauded Agee for his "misgivings at being a spy and a stranger, his refusal to submit to the categories of sociology or the devices of drama." "I feel sure this is a great book," said Lionel Trilling; "nine out of every ten pages are superb. Agee has a sensibility so precise, so unremitting, that it is sometimes appalling." Alfred Kazin called *A Death in the Family* "an utterly individual and original book, and it is the work of a writer whose power with English words can make you gasp." Robert Lowell said, "I add Agee's death to his hero's and can't forget the epitaph."

Dwight Macdonald left the finest comment on the whole man: "Yes, I was very fond of Agee and I think he was fond of me, too. We liked each other very much and we respected each other, which is perhaps equally important, you know. He was pretty much of a bum in many ways. He didn't wash very much, his clothes were filthy, and he was very bad sexually, to say the least—you know, a loose liver. And he drank too much and had a lot of faults. But I must say, he's one of the few people that I've ever met that I would consider, without any question, a genius. Like Auden, Eliot, people like that, without any question."

███

Agee demanded more freedom than most of his contemporaries while expecting to accomplish less than any of them. Measured against the breed of writers who emerged in the 1950s, his prose seems static, as if caught between equally valid perceptions, or immobilized in the bereaved perspective of his boyhood. Unlike the new narcissists, however, he did not exploit his subjects, or betray his ex-wives or his parents for the sake of Art and Ambition. He never forced the grief of his subjects to undergo the brutalities of action or the humiliations of analysis. His oscillating style managed to be realistic and tender at the same time, to get love and death into view rather than sex and violence. "Each individual existence" he wrote in his introduction to Walker Evans's collection of subway photographs, *Many Are Called*, "is as matchless as a thumbprint or a snowflake. Each wears garments which of themselves are exquisitely subtle uniforms and badges of their being. Each carries in the postures of his body, in his hands, in his face, in the eyes, the signatures of a time and a place in the world upon a creature for whom the name immortal soul is one mild and vulgar metaphor."

In his sensitivity to the privacy of the soul, to the disquiet of modern experience, Agee confides the dignity of human emotion, and teaches us to detect the false notes in posterity's trumpets. In this spirit may we remember him; by our furies, rather than by any successes that may be borne by them.

WHAT HAPPENED TO
SEX SCANDALS?

"**A**ny man familiar with public life realizes the foul gossip which ripples just under the surface about almost every public man, and especially about every President," observed Theodore Roosevelt in 1913. Varieties of "foul gossip" have plagued officeholders from the founding of the Republic to the present day, as Roosevelt suggested. Yet the nature, effects, and reach of gossip have undergone curious and striking transformations over the years. Think of one especially common topic of discussion: a politician's reputation for sexual rectitude. In the early republic and throughout the nineteenth century, political culture subjected the sexual character of officeholders to close, steady, and often unflattering scrutiny. As Roosevelt said, most voters believed a man of virtue to be "the only safe depository of public trust." By the beginning of the twentieth century, however, revelations of sexual turpitude among prominent elected officials had begun to disappear from public life. Thomas Jefferson, Andrew Jackson, Grover Cleveland, and other members of the nineteenth-century political elite negotiated their reputations among a broad array of publics. In the new era, Warren G. Harding, Franklin D. Roosevelt, and John F. Kennedy benefited from a more circumspect pattern in political speech. Theodore Roosevelt's remark is doubly useful in this respect. If "foul gossip" could still circulate in 1913, it had already started to travel, not openly, but rather "just under the surface" of public life.

What explains this transformation? Historians often observe that during the first decades of the century, gossip, confession, and expo-sure arose as distinctive attributes of mass communication, corroding

Victorian modesty in virtually every arena of American life. What Rochelle Gurstein calls a "repeal of reticence" helps define this era and its aftermath. Why, then, could leading figures in American politics expect political culture to spare their sexual transgressions from the popular scrutiny endured by their predecessors? In examining this, the guiding problem of the essay, I consider and reject a number of possible explanations and finally settle on two key developments: changes to the ideology and practice of professional journalism and the psychology of insulation that accompanied the emergence of a newly nationalized political elite at the dawn of the last century.

▮▮▮

Criticism of the sexual rectitude of politicians first surfaced as a regular part of American public life in the acrimonious milieu of the 1780s and 1790s. During those transitional decades, while John Adams and other leading officials entreated the electorate for "Decency, and Respect, and Veneration…for Persons in Authority," older notions of deference and reticence began to recede. In their place emerged a fierce brand of political combat that regarded personal morality as a legitimate field of battle. James Callender, in his *History of the United States for 1796,* ruminated about the "real character of some people;" charges he made elsewhere drew public attention to the supposed extramarital affairs of Alexander Hamilton and Thomas Jefferson. Personalized attacks of this sort provoked bitter objections. The Federalist-inspired Sedition Act (1798)—the early republic's most notable attempt to quell clamorous political dialogue—treated "scandalous and malicious writing or writings against" any elected official as treasonous behavior. Even staunch defenders of a free press bemoaned the frequency of personal invective. "If by the *Liberty of the Press* were understood merely the Liberty of discussing the Propriety of Public Measures and political opinions, let us have as much of it as you please," Benjamin Franklin wrote in 1789, petitioning the Pennsylvania legislature for a civil libel statute. "But if it means the Liberty of affronting, calumniating, and defaming one another, I, for my part…shall cheerfully consent to exchange my *Liberty* of Abusing others for the Privilege of not being abus'd myself."

Nevertheless, American politics relentlessly scrutinized the personal morality of politicians for much of the next century, and sexual misbehavior became a favorite topic. A well-orchestrated campaign of defamation marked the election of 1800—the first modern presidential contest—as Federalists furiously circulated tales of "Mr. Jefferson's Congo Harem." Opponents of Andrew Jackson in 1828 and Grover Cleveland in 1884 likewise questioned the fidelity and chastity of the candidates. Few influential figures of the nineteenth century escaped such imputations. William Henry Harrison was supposed to have fathered several illegitimate children—the *Ohio Statesman* said he was "the seducer of a young and unprotected female"—and John Quincy Adams allegedly "attempted to make use of a beautiful girl to seduce the passion of the [Russian] Emperor Alexander and sway him to political purposes." Adams, echoing Franklin, complained about this "new form of slander—one of the thousand malicious lies which outvenom all the worms of Nile, and are circulated in every part of the country in newspapers and pamphlets." Seemingly every politician claimed to be "peculiarly an object of persecution"—as Alexander Hamilton groused about James Callender's charges—or, like Harrison, affected astonishment at the sheer number and variety of canards. "I am the most persecuted and calumniated person now living," he complained during the 1840 presidential campaign.

"To the European, a public officer represents a superior force: to an American, he represents a right," explained Alexis de Tocqueville, who lamented the tendency of journalists to "assail the character of individuals, to track them into private life, and disclose all their weaknesses and vices." Lady Emmeline Stuart Wortley, writing in 1851, made a similar observation. The American "abuse of the authorities and people in office is beyond all idea violent," she wrote. "The most unmerciful vituperations are poured forth against some of their most eminent men; *really* if you did not see their names you would sometimes think they were speaking of the most atrocious criminals."

What explains this close attention to the personal character of politicians? In part, the highly personalized inflection of political speech emanated from the partisanship of nineteenth-century public life. By the antebellum era partisanship had become the "first commandment" of American politics and had found its greatest expression in the mass-based parties, according to Michael McGerr's *The Decline of Popular Politics.* Dominating elections and furnishing a widely shared lexicon for political participation, the parties typically favored "aggressive, demonstrative, contentious, and often vicious" techniques of politicking. In this milieu, personal abuse was a natural weapon, and libelous editorials—as an expression of partisan fealty—adorned the nation's party newspapers.

That parties often waged ferocious elections, however, does not explain their choice of weapons. Why did the character of politicians matter in the first place? Why were personal scruples, such as marital fidelity, considered legitimate topics for open discussion? If the emergence of a discordant, competitive party system guaranteed extensive circulation to tales of moral iniquity, the scrutiny of personal life stemmed from a conviction that transcended partisan loyalties: that a just and orderly polity required evidence of personal virtue among its elected leaders.

Like so many other habits of American political culture, this impetus to demand virtue in leaders derived from multiple traditions. American republicanism—a readily available vocabulary from which a wide array of political actors drew—regarded solid moral character as a *sine qua non* of good government. Repudiating older, hierarchical notions of authority and service, republicans made personal virtue a foundation of representation and insisted that only persons of exemplary rectitude should occupy positions of power. They believed that without personal integrity their leaders would not withstand the temptation of corruption and the pursuit of narrow self-interest. Virtue, then, facilitated tasks widely considered vital to the protection of freedom in consent-based societies: warding off corruption, checking tyranny, ensuring an enlightened citizenry, and thereby promoting the general welfare.

"We have just been through the U.S. and with the exception of Louisiana and Georgia, we saw nothing but fraud, violence and oppression—distress of all sorts, and vice the most abandoned," wrote Anne Royall, whose national gossip sheet, *Paul Pry,* achieved a wide and uneasy readership among antebellum congressmen. "The President, we fancy, does not pry into these things as we do, though he need not go out of Washington to find ignorance, vice and distress." For Royall and other republicans, scrutinizing moral character and exposing unscrupulousness constituted a public good, a guarantor against moral decay. "Take warning, gentlemen," Royall cautioned in 1831, "I have the honor to be the public's most devoted friend."

Evangelical Protestantism also persuaded nineteenth-century voters to seek for public service men of esteemed character. "Human governments are plainly recognized in the Bible as a part of the moral government of God," insisted the revivalist Charles Grandison Finney. "It is nonsense to admit that Christians are under an obligation to obey human government, and still have nothing to do with the choice of those who shall govern." Following Finney, nineteenth-century apostles of energetic religion urged upon voters "honest, well-known men of sound morals." Placing the idea of the sacred covenant near the center of American politics, these self-proclaimed "Christian patriots" brought pressure to bear on elected officials who neglected virtues such as chastity and self-restraint. Richard M. Johnson, for instance, was denied the formal nomination for the vice presidency in 1840 due to fears that his unusual marital arrangement—Johnson lived openly with his mulatto common-law wife—would offend not only proponents of racial inequality but also the many voters for whom religious morality constituted the first and final criterion for elevating the citizens to public service.

Politicians who disdained religious views might also face direct opposition, for throughout the 1850s increasing numbers of evangelicals stood for public office. Self-rule, evangelicals cried, would ultimately become impossible without virtuous leaders. "If general intelligence, public and private virtue, sink to that point below which self-control becomes practically impossible, we must fall back into monarchy, limited or absolute; or into civil or military despotism," maintained

Finney, forging a potent synthesis of republican and evangelical senti-ment. "This is as certain as that God governs the world."

Politicians of both parties heeded such admonitions and present-ed themselves to voters as men of sexual virtue, honor, integrity, and good judgment. The growth of political society, however, soon intro-duced an awkward problem: if good character conferred legitimacy upon authority, as evangelicals and republicans each contended, then what prevented officeholders from wearing virtue as a disguise? By the antebellum period, America's increasingly anonymous society had made *reputation* an unstable concept, easy to counterfeit. "In order to secure my character and credit as a tradesman," Benjamin Franklin had written in a famous passage in his *Autobiography,* "I took care not only to be in *reality* industrious and frugal, but to avoid all appearances to the contrary." That wily politicians might adopt Franklin's distinction between appearance and reality to become inscrutable confidence men did not seem to trouble him. Nineteenth-century Americans, however, met the promise of self-making with anxiety, fearing that public figures would cultivate fraudulent images of moral probity. Davy Crockett importuned the readers of his popular biography of Martin Van Buren to recognize that Van Buren was "not the man he is cracked up to be; and if he is made president of the United States, he will have reached a place to which he is not entitled, either by sense or sincerity."

Voters relieved their anxiety over the specter of the politician as dissembling confidence man by calling upon a vigorously democratic political culture. Nineteenth-century Americans filtered republican and Protestant world views through a lens of popular democracy that required all claims, public and private, to confront "the broad light of day," as Tocqueville wrote. Popular democracy, wary of usurpers and contemptuous of deference, everywhere manifested an "insistence on transparency" and refused to countenance politi-cal secrecy. This helps account for the widespread appeal of such writers as Anne Royall and the non-partisan humorist Seba Smith, whose popular Jack Downing series aimed to expose the "strange doings" and "ridiculous" affects of officials in power. As Herman

Melville and Edgar Allan Poe probed the mysterious underworld of urban culture, Royall, Smith, and their colleagues inspected sincerity among politicians.

The repudiation of secrecy by popular democrats also explains why alarms about hypocrisy nearly always accompanied allegations of immoral conduct, and why charges of illegitimacy and adultery (by definition sins of deceit and seduction) occupied pride of place in this era. Republicanism and evangelical Protestantism demanded virtue among leaders, but the active, intensely public search for sullied sexual character derived from the democratic incarnations of these traditions.

■■■

The hunt for adulterers, illegitimate fathers, and other moral miscreants in political life proceeded apace in the last half of the century. Henry Ward Beecher discovered as much when Victoria Woodhull divulged the politically active minister's dalliances with Elizabeth Tilton. As this scandal erupted in the early 1870s, charges of hypocrisy and immorality poured forth from an affronted press. Even before the disclosure of Beecher's transgressions horrified his followers and gladdened his enemies, the editors of the *Nation* denounced America's "insane culture of publicity" and lamented its tendency to treat public figures as tawdry objects of abuse. The magazine soon joined the *North American Review,* the *Forum,* and other organs of the 1880s and 1890s in righteous protest against the invasive journalism that gripped these decades.

Private character, despite this dissent, continued to serve as a useful implement of partisan battle, especially among those disinclined to presume the legitimacy of political authority. In *Caesar's Column,* Ignatius Donnelly's 1890 novel, the narrative pivots around the concubine of the Prince of Cabano—the president of the Council of the Plutocracy—whose personal moral corruption constitutes a sure measure of his political wickedness. At the book's conclusion, Donnelly signifies Caesar's own moral enervation by having him take mistresses. "'This is my palace. I am a king! Look-a-there,' he said, with a roll and a leer, pointing over his shoulder at the shrinking and terrified women; 'ain't they beauties—hic—all mine—every one of 'em'."

In 1892, Tom Watson, Populist congressman from Georgia, ignited a furor by mocking the pretensions of rectitude proffered by his colleagues in the House of Representatives. Relating "their capacity to live in idleness" to their need to "gratify sensual pleasures," Watson reported that "drunken members have reeled about the aisles—a disgrace to the Republic. Drunken speakers have debated grave issues on the Floor and in the midst of maudlin rumblings have been heard to ask, 'Mr. Speaker, where was I at?'"

In the election of 1900, Prohibitionist party literature imputed sexual corruption and other "exhibitions of moral filth" to Democratic and Republican leaders alike. Delegates to the Republican presidential convention, charged one exposé, trafficked with "scarlet women much in evidence," as prostitutes in "suspiciously scanty attire...found a ready, even eager, patronage." "The party which chooses such men for its representatives, and which is led not to say 'bossed' by men of such character, is not worthy of the confidence or support of intelligent men."

The major parties returned aspersions in kind. Although Republicans were more likely to target offenders against sexual morality, some prominent Democrats also acknowledged the connection between private virtue and political legitimacy. The *Albany Argus* wrote in 1844, "The sentiment that a man pure and upright in his private character, is the only safe depository of public trust, is one that commends itself to the American People. It is obvious that the vices and immoralities of private life will be carried into the public administration, and that one who has been notoriously immoral and reckless in his personal gratifications, cannot be less reckless and selfish in his public capacity."

A half-century later, William C. P. Breckinridge, legislator from Kentucky and rising star in the Democratic Party, renewed this proclamation. "Pure homes make pure governments," he once instructed pupils at an all-female college. "Chastity is the foundation, the corner-stone of human society." Unfortunately for him, Madeline Pollard—his longtime mistress and the mother of his illegitimate children—betrayed the hollowness of this advice when she sued him for breach of promise in 1893. The trial was a humiliating national spectacle for Breckinridge. Still, the congressman determined to run for reelection the next year, prompting Susan B. Anthony to predict that "exposed and confessed unchastity won't win." She was correct. Prior to the 1894 election, the influential Breckinridge faced little opposition for the Democratic nomination. This time his bid attracted a list of contenders, and the election generated the largest turnout ever for a primary in that district.

Like Republicans, the Democrats did not hesitate to attack rivals, internal and external, for iniquity. Nor did they fail to trumpet the personal integrity of deserving candidates, as the 1884 presidential election indicates. That campaign, in fact, amply demonstrates the convergence of partisan, republican, religious, and democratic exigencies around the notion of sexual virtue. Throughout his brief career in politics, the Democrats' nominee, Grover Cleveland, had deliberately projected moral uprightness and unassailable honesty. The bachelor son of a minister, "Grover the Good" had devoted ample attention to questions of professional ethics, capturing the governorship of New York in 1882 with a pledge to end the corruption of urban machines. Two years later, as he prepared to battle Republican James G. Blaine for the presidency, campaign biographies emphasized Cleveland's "indubitable strength of character." "There is but little fiction in his make-up," assured Deschler Welch's *Stephen Grover Cleveland: A Sketch of His Life* (1884).

On July 24, 1884, a minister from Buffalo imputed to Cleveland "habitual immoralities with women." Writing in the *Buffalo Evening Telegraph,* the Reverend George Ball claimed that Cleveland, in addition to strutting around town "beastly drunk," had once made the acquaintance of a "beautiful, virtuous, and intelligent young lady" named Maria Halpin, who worked in the cloak department of a Buffalo department store. Cleveland "won her confidence and finally seduced her." Halpin, Ball said, became pregnant, but Cleveland withdrew his promise to marry her, then "employed two detectives and a doctor of bad repute to spirit the woman away and dispose of the child."

These sensational charges were quickly transmitted throughout the nation, eliciting heated commentary from ministers, partisans, and independents. Cleveland's "election would argue a low state of morals among the people, and be a burning shame and never-to-be-forgotten disgrace to the nation," said the *Independent* soon after the news broke. "No man with such a private character as is shown in respect to him is fit to fill any office in the gift of the people." Sympathetic clergymen such as Henry Ward Beecher conducted investigations into Cleveland's character, while others fulminated against him in pulpits in major cities.

The Halpin affair generated an unprecedented number of letters to suffragist Lucy Stone's *Woman's Journal*. Stone herself lamented the "revolting facts" and insisted that "he should be dropped at once." "In such a contest women must be opposed, at all other cost, to that which is the destruction of the home," she wrote. "They know with unerring instinct that the purity and safety of the home means purity and safety to the state and nation."

The scandal made great political theater. Republican stalwarts branded Cleveland a "moral leper," chanted "Ma, Ma, Where's My Pa?" and pushed carriages containing baby dolls in city parades.

Democratic party operatives retaliated by circulating a claim that Blaine's wife had given birth to her son only three months after the couple's marriage. Already battling accusations of cupidity, Blaine was now asked to answer an allegation about his sexual rectitude. As the Democratic *Indianapolis Sentinel* fumed, "there is hardly an intelligent man in the country who has not heard that James G. Blaine betrayed the girl whom he married and then only married her at the muzzle of a shotgun."

The election turned on the question of sincerity. In exposing Cleveland's "habitual immoralities with women," Reverend George

Ball suggested that the Democrats had attempted to foist a fictional reputation upon the electorate. "Since his candidacy is being pushed on the assumption of irreproachable morals," Ball wrote, "it would be criminal to allow the virtuous to vote for so vile a man as thus under a false impression that he is pure and honorable." But Cleveland's candor persuaded enough voters to secure his victory in November. On July 23, 1884, he telegraphed a message to his managers in Buffalo, admitting a rendezvous with Halpin and confessing that he might have fathered a child to her. (The rest of the gossip—especially the detail about the insane asylum—he emphatically denied.) "Whatever you do," implored the telegram, "tell the truth." The Blaine forces kept the Halpin story alive until the eve of the election, but Cleveland's admission restored his credibility.

███

On November 13, 1884, Grover Cleveland wrote to a friend about the uproar over Maria Halpin. "I intend to cultivate the Christian virtue of charity toward all men except the dirty class that defiled themselves with filthy scandal and Ballism," he swore. "I don't believe God will ever forgive them and I am determined not to do so." Cleveland held firm to his promise, flaying the press with mordant criticism in office, and indeed throughout the remainder of his life. The Halpin affair, however, was the last major scandal of its kind for more than a century. Sexual rectitude remained a topic for open debate well into the 1890s, but willingness to expose the unsavory habits of influential politicians yielded to a new mood in American political culture—a return of reticence. Partisan rivals and "paul pry" journalists continued to gossip uncharitably about Cleveland, yet both averted their gaze from his successor, Benjamin Harrison, whose moral accounts suffered no significant public scrutiny. The aloof William McKinley also enjoyed a gossip-free administration. So, too, did William Howard Taft and Woodrow Wilson escape from the discomfort of debating their sexual peccadilloes. Cartoonists poked fun at Taft's impressive girth, but no major allegations against his sexual character surfaced in the press. Wilson's tenure in the White House occasioned several gossip-worthy personal events, including the death of his first wife and his remarriage to Edith Bolling Galt. In 1911, unflattering rumors about his amorous connection to Mary Allen Peck were "whispered about the corridors of the Democratic National Convention," as the journalist David Lawrence remembered. Speculation about Peck snaked through Washington salons and convention corridors, and Wilson prepared for an embarrassing scandal by drafting an apologetic memorandum about his "passage of folly and gross impertinence," for which he was "deeply ashamed and repentant." Yet the memorandum was unnecessary. No one trafficked openly in the Peck matter. Does this constitute a major departure from nineteenth-century habits of scrutiny? The case of Warren G. Harding demonstrates the change. At the 1920 presidential nominating convention, Republican operative George Harvey asked Harding to a private meeting, where Harvey asked the candidate about his personal habits. "We think you may be nominated tomorrow," warned Harvey. "Before acting finally we think you should tell us...whether there is anything that might be brought against you that would embarrass the party, any impediment that might disqualify you or make you inexpedient."

Early in Harding's political career, he had embarked on a romance with Carrie Phillips, wife of a Marion, Ohio, department store owner and a family friend. In 1917, while he continued his assignations with Phillips, Harding found a second paramour, an unmarried eighteen-year-old woman named Nan Britton. In 1919, Britton bore him a daughter. According to biographer Francis Russell, gossip about Harding's "two women" traveled about the Capitol and among the salons of Washington society. By the standards of the nineteenth century, the candidate was ripe for exposure. Yet, upon returning from a mere ten minutes of solitary reflection, Harding answered George Harvey with a resolute no, clearing the way for the nomination.

The decision proved politically safe, for neither journalists nor rival Democrats disclosed his philandering to voters, though both ruminated privately about the matter. One major magazine profile even claimed that the Hardings projected "a certain idyllic quality that happily married partnerships have." (The author neglected to mention that both Florence Harding and James Cox, the Democratic nominee, were once divorced.) Harding suffered multiple posthumous indignities: Nan Britton wrote a widely circulated exposé, *The President's Daughter* (1927), and the writer Samuel Hopkins Adams and the investigator Gaston Means issued scathing attacks on other examples of the administration's ethical laxity. Yet during his entire term in office, voters did not read anything about Harding's adultery. The charges, and more general suggestions of turpitude, waited for his demise and the disgrace of his administration. Even then, the dead president's detractors became targets of state repression, and reluctant reviewers of Britton's book discerned no important lessons in her tale. H. L. Mencken, who routinely decried the "progressive degeneration of the honesty and honour" of American politicians, admitted his indifference to their sexual peccadilloes. "This tale, I confess, does not interest me greatly."

Why did political rivals and newspapermen keep quiet about Harding's affairs? Why did Wilson's relationship with Peck fail to complicate his ambitions? Those who wished to discredit either man might have appealed to the tradition in American politics of attacking disreputable sexual character. And a public discussion of adultery would have flattered the irreverent temper of the early century. Tabloid newspapers and respectable publications, each in their own way, paraded the raiments of private life before readers. "Wherever one turned the Greenwich Village ideas were making their way," Malcolm Cowley wrote of the 1920s. "Even the *Saturday Evening Post* was feeling their influence. It allowed drinking, petting, and unfaithfulness to be mentioned in the stories it published." Vice societies and censorship efforts foundered, and sex reformers inaugurated a franker discussion of intimate matters during these years. Movie stars such as Douglas Fairbanks and Rudolph Valentino, sports heroes such as Babe Ruth, and glamorous religious figures such as Sister Aimee Semple McPherson watched as an ethos of what Ann Douglas has called "terrible honesty" devoured their privacy. Babe Ruth made fewer enemies than either Woodrow Wilson or Warren Harding yet grew exasperated at coverage of his turbulent sex life. "What really gets me sore is those stories about me and women, and the pictures," the slugger once scolded a pack of New York City reporters. "I can take the baseball stories, but can't you lay off the woman stuff? I'd be very much obliged if you boys stuck to my baseball troubles and left my marital affairs alone."

If the river of articles, speeches, and pamphlets probing for hypocrisy and immorality among politicians of national reputation slowed by the 1920s, it largely stopped by the New Deal years. Franklin Roosevelt ordered a special car to take his mistress, Lucy Mercer Rutherford, to his 1932 inauguration. More than a dozen years later, Rutherford was present at the president's bedside when he died. Correspondents, Republican publishers, and others traded gossip about the relationship but made no mention of either Rutherford or Missy LeHand—another of the president's paramours—during Roosevelt's time in office. The *friendship* between Rutherford and Roosevelt did not become public knowledge until 1949, the *romance* not until 1966.

By the time John F. Kennedy ascended to the presidency, reticence had become a fixed principle of American political exchange, according to the journalist Jules Witcover: "The accepted attitude was that a political figure's private life was his own business unless it affected the performance of his public duties, and, therefore, reporters did not go out of their way to learn about that private life. Only if a senator fell down drunk on the floor of the Senate might that fact be reported. If another senator had a mistress on the side and continued to do his job, the press figured—so what?" Kennedy, known in these circles for his womanizing, enjoyed protection both from the national press corps and from political rivals, who sometimes attempted to document his liaisons but who never organized a public campaign to discredit him—even though, as the Catholic husband of a widely esteemed First Lady, the president was doubly vulnerable to exposure. In 1963, the Profumo sex scandal devastated Harold Macmillan's Conservative government in Great Britain. By contrast, President Kennedy's assignations with Judith Campbell Exner, Marilyn Monroe, Ellen Rometsch, and Durie Malcolm remained secrets, their concealment central to the popular image of Camelot. As the 1884 election of Grover Cleveland marked the culmination of one pattern in political speech, so did Kennedy's tenure in the White House mark the culmination of another.

∎∎∎

What explains this transformation? Did evidence of good character cease to matter as a prerequisite for political office? Historian Warren Susman has charged public culture in the early twentieth century with "somewhat less interest in moral imperatives." In the 1900s and 1910s, Susman says, a "culture of personality" began to displace an older "culture of character," as traits such as magnetism, attractiveness, and self-realization began to command attention. Other historians, making corollary arguments, have maintained that the very idea of virtue underwent dramatic transformations throughout the nineteenth and early twentieth centuries. Once a masculine endowment, virtue, they argue, found its provenance in women's "separate sphere." Still others insist that republican aspirations for a shared public morality diminished during the late Gilded Age, owing to the brutality of the Civil War, persistent economic and political corruption, and the steady rationalization of social and intellectual life. According to these scholars, virtue became an attribute for individual, *private* display.

These claims remind us that the notion of sexual virtue does not itself make a stable variable. Then again, did the advent of *personality* mark the end of virtue as a category of public discourse, or depoliticize *character*? Did politicians really affect indifference to their reputation for sexual rectitude? In fact, they understood that rectitude still mattered to many voters at election time and accordingly continued to present themselves as men of "impeccable moral character," "unostentatious piety," and "sturdy republican virtue," as one study of campaign biographies published between 1824 and 1960 has concluded. Theodore Roosevelt regarded the presidency as a morally informed "bully pulpit" and asserted that only an

Individual "foundation of character" could lead to "national great-ness." "No man can lead a public career really worth leading...if he himself is vulnerable in his private character," Roosevelt wrote. "I do not for one moment admit that political morality is different from private morality, that a promise made on the stump differs from a promise made in private life."

An abstemious personal disposition and a moralistic public policy operated symbiotically for Woodrow Wilson. Calvin Coolidge, the "Puritan in Babylon," crafted a personal reputation that contrasted favorably with Harding's. In 1928, Republican operatives floated rumors that Al Smith had been seen drunk in public and portrayed their own candidate, Herbert Hoover, as a man of "honesty" and "integrity" who would "protect your home." Franklin Roosevelt's fatherly image worked in similar fashion.

Good sexual character lingered as a talisman in the public lan-guage of American political culture. Why else did the Republican National Committee offer to dispatch Carrie Phillips, one of Har-ding's paramours, to Europe with twenty thousand dollars in hush money? Why else did Franklin Roosevelt, an "amiable tyrant" who ordered "the boldest of [reporters] to go stand in the corner if they asked questions he didn't like"—as James Reston complained—seek and extract assurances that certain sensitive, personal subjects would remain inviolable? To carry the point into the Cold War period, the recurring importance of personal virtue explains the logic directing the machinations of J. Edgar Hoover, who counted blackmail among his cache of weapons against rival politicians and nonconformists such as Martin Luther King Jr. Upon what foundation did this leverage rest, if not the expectation of sexual virtue? A charming personality might help persuade audiences, but respectability underwrote the legitimacy of the glad-handing politician and the dissenter alike.

Does respect for privacy explain the return of reticence about sex? Reformers in the late nineteenth century appealed to privacy in their opposition to public gossip. Prominent figures such as E. L. Godkin, Henry Adams, and Charles Eliot Norton wanted protection from the boorish stares of the "ignorant and barbaric multitudes," as Norton once wrote. Imbued with contempt for popular politics, these reformers argued that disclosing the moral transgressions of public figures polluted political life and conflated "all distinctions between wholesome, necessary intelligence and that which corrupts and contaminates," as an editorialist in the *North American Review* wrote. Reading scandal in newspapers was a "bad habit," a "mild form of mania which needs regulation and control as much as other petty vices of human nature." This agitation against what *The Nation* called the "anarchy of journalism" became increasingly influential. Privacy as a concept in civil law—whose violation was a tort—won adherents in the late 1890s, when a widely read paper by Samuel Warren and Louis Brandeis, "The Right to Privacy," brought the matter of unwanted newspaper publicity to the attention of the perturbed classes.

Privacy, however, was practically unenforceable, since pressing charges against violations only intensified exposure. And libel law—still under the control of states—remained contradictory and confusing until 1964, when it was nationalized. The threat of prosecution for libel must have influenced individual situations. But as a guide to shifts in public culture it returns few reliable clues. In 1941 Curtis D. MacDougall, a lecturer in journalism at Northwestern University, stated that "almost no lawyers specialize in libel law, few editors and publishers are clear regarding it, individuals who actually have been libeled do not understand their rights and state laws are not uniform but inconsistent, vague, and confusing." Even among the national press corps the effectiveness of libel law was unclear. The most daring and the most sued of all Washington-based political reporters in the twentieth century, Drew Pearson, lost only one libel case in his long career and professed, with good cause, never to fear the courtroom. Neither libel statutes nor the privacy tort could have generated a nationwide trend toward reticence.

In fact, reports about certain personal activities of national politicians *intensified* after the 1890s. Anticipating coverage of the

Kennedy family, the adventures of Theodore Roosevelt and his energetic children appeared often in the press. When Alice Roosevelt, the president's eldest daughter, married Congressman Nicholas Longworth in 1906, details of the ceremony decorated newspapers and periodicals across the nation. Everywhere "dogged by reporters," Alice Roosevelt noticed "inquisitive crowds following when I went shopping; to some extent the sort of thing a royalty or a movie star endures, or enjoys." "But I suppose we were fair game for the press of the day," she wrote in her memoir, *Crowded Hours*. Roosevelt brooked unrelenting newspaper coverage with equanimity. Others found the nakedness of political life more disconcerting. Woodrow Wilson's second wife, Edith, confessed in her memoir that "the terrible thought of publicity" almost persuaded her to reject the president's marriage proposal.

Why, then, did indiscretions about sex retreat from view? One explanation centers on the metamorphosis of American journalism. Under steady attack from anti-party elites and from Progressive Era reformers, the distinctive style of nineteenth-century public life began to deteriorate after the 1880s. Partisanship remained part of electioneering in the new era, but the fresh notion of *independence* began to discredit unswerving party loyalties, as proponents of a more intellectualized, educative brand of politics undermined customs. In seeking to elaborate a more rational foundation for political life, reformers launched a broad-based assault on popular politics that weakened the social and moral function of the parties. Democrats and Republicans retained their grip on the electoral process while party machinery fell to specialists and experts. As part of this broad disaggregation, reporters and editors broke free from their partisan moorings, established journalism as an autonomous profession, and thereby ended the party monopolies on political information.

"How far can we go in turning newspaper enterprise from a haphazard trade into a disciplined profession?" wondered Walter Lippmann in 1920. "Quite far, I imagine, for it is altogether unthinkable that a society like ours should remain forever dependent upon untrained accidental witnesses." Reticence about the immoralities of political figures first acquired concerted support in the professionalization of journalism. Ethical codes were "the heart of the whole matter," according to Joseph Pulitzer. In 1910, Kansas editors—the first to articulate ethical maxims—insisted that "however prominent the principals, offenses against private morality should never receive first page position, and their details should be eliminated as much as possible." The *Brooklyn Daily Eagle* instructed that, when writing obituaries, one should "not emphasize unfortunate incidents in the lives of well reputed persons," while in Oregon another group maintained that "the reputations of men and women are sacred in nature, and not to be torn down lightly."

The American Society of Newspaper Editors (ASNE) crafted the most influential set of professional guidelines. In 1923 the newly formed group called for "fair play," which meant "a newspaper should not publish unofficial charges affecting reputation or moral character without opportunity given to the accused to be heard." Furthermore, "a newspaper should not invade private rights or feelings without sure warrant of public right as distinguished from public curiosity." Similar versions of fair play appeared in nearly every guide to professional newspaper practice in the 1910s and 1920s.

Sentiment for codes had been building for decades. But why did prescriptions of fair play achieve such a broad accord in this period? Insulation for "well reputed persons" emerged as a reflection of professional journalism's renunciation of popular politics. Beginning in the early decades of the twentieth century, and especially after the bewildering vagaries of public opinion during World War I, a consensus of democratic realists formed among social scientists, philosophers, businessmen, and reform-minded intellectuals. The complexities of industrial society, insisted realists, had thrown into sharp relief the inherently limited nature of political knowledge. Whereas the United States had modeled its democratic institutions on small communities, in the larger communities of the modern industrial world a "twilight zone"—as Lippmann wrote in his 1925 book, *The Phantom Public*—obscured differences between fact and propaganda, rendering public opinion irrational and, without proper regulation, misguided. Hence the need for experts to gather, interpret, and disseminate political information.

Led by Lippmann, leaders in journalism hewed closely to the realist position, often distinguishing between "giving the public what it wants" and "giving the public what it should have." Critics such as the writer John Macy regarded newspaper readers as dullards. "The Reader, the Public is mute, if not inglorious," sneered Macy's entry in *Civilization in the United States,* "and accepts uncritically what the daily press provides." Gerald Johnson, a well-known editorial writer for the *Baltimore Sun,* insisted that "the American reader of newspapers, that is, almost everybody, is a duffer, so far as the newspaper is concerned, uncritical, docile, and only meekly incredulous."

Others, sharing Macy and Johnson's judgments, also warned of the dangers of public opinion. In his textbook on editorial writing, M. Lyle Spencer, president of the University of Washington, advised that "a writer must always take the hostility of the mob public into consideration. Its wrath is intense and destructive. Like fire, it knows no limits or reason. One who has been burned by it once, never forgets. In a period of intense excitement or great upheaval an editorial running counter to its emotions may mean destruction." Washington Gladden's 1915 essay—published in the collection *The Coming Newspaper*—asked journalists to "avoid exaggeration" and "to cultivate moderate and rational modes of expression." For, when provoked, public opinion becomes hostage to "emotional mutations in which it ceases to be opinion and becomes mere sentiment, unorganized, highly volatile and inflammable, keeping no steady course but, like the wind, blowing where it listeth, possessing tremendous force, but having no assignable direction." "It is pretty clear," fretted Gladden, a widely esteemed Congregationalist clergyman, "that the crowd self is getting to be a portentous figure in our democratic civilization."

As democratic realists, editors and reporters assigned themselves the "very great obligation" of managing the opinions of voters. "No people have ever progressed morally who did not have conceptions of right impressed upon them by moral leadership," wrote Casper Yost, editor of the *St. Louis Globe-Democrat* and first president of the ASNE, in a remark typical of his formative generation of professional journalists. To the question of whether "giving the public what it wants" remained a defensible standard for editors, every respondent at a 1914 symposium answered in the negative. "The editor," admonished the clergyman and religious journalist Lyman Abbott, "is, or ought to be, a public teacher." Another conferee struck an even more telling analogy, comparing newspaper readers to children whose puerile tastes required stern discipline by figures of authority: "It is simply up to the newspaper man to sort out that demand very carefully and make up his mind what particular feature of the demand he is going to supply." "To protect the people from themselves, to point out their errors, and urge rectification, is the true mission of journalism," maintained George Harvey, editor of *Harper's Weekly,* at Yale University in 1908. "The master journalist must have the stability of purpose and coolness of judgment"; his "aim must be to uplift humanity, not to profit by its degradation." Surveying recent developments in the field, Harvey seemed pleased. "The journalist has become the accepted and most potent guide of the masses," he remarked. "Great strides have been made in American journalism. The asperities of to-day seem innocuous when compared with those of the good old times . . . when [John] Jay was anathematized as a scoundrel and [Thomas] Jefferson as an atheist and a satyr."

Walter Lippmann, Lyman Abbott, Gerald Johnson, George Harvey, Washington Gladden, and Casper Yost viewed one another as custodians of the unmannered masses, moral and political cynosures authorized to guide a wayward political culture. Once, evangelicals and republicans appealed to the populace to monitor the morality of political elites. Now, political elites were charged with the discipline of the populace. Notice how Washington Gladden mixes the old evangelical concern for morality and self-control with newer anxieties about the "mob mind." "One of the great duties of all public teachers and leaders is to discourage all those crazes and fads and rages in which people exchange reason for passion, and judgment for imitation," Gladden wrote in *The Coming Newspaper.* "Whatever tends to develop the mob mind tends to make government by public opinion impossible. Whatever tends to keep people reasonable, and thoughtful, and self-controlled, and fair-minded is cultivating in the public mind those qualities and habits on which we must rely." Reticence emerged as part of a broad operation to protect the workings of government from the sort of scrutiny that characterized the popular politics of the nineteenth century.

If reticence originated as part of an ideology of insulation, and, correspondingly, of a concentration of power among early-twentieth-century elites whose authority rested substantially upon their ability to re-monopolize political knowledge, it proved an ideal especially serviceable for journalism. The promise of reticence permitted elite reporters to get closer to the instruments of government power. Correspondents who endorsed "fair play" demonstrated a willingness to keep secrets from their readers. For reporters such as Mark Sullivan, who recalled that during the latter half of his career "practically all my associations, both personal and those that went with my work, were with public men," earning the confidence of sources meant protecting them. Prominent nineteenth-century newsmen also traveled in the shadows of big political men. But associations such as the National Press Club—established in 1908 frankly to promote "friendly intercourse" between reporters and the "Great Names" of American politics—naturalized *quid pro quo* arrangements. A *Washington Post* reporter remembered, happily, that "the people who made the news came more and more as time passed to the clubhouse and talked more freely than they would anywhere else." Behind the facade of objective professionalism, new journalistic organizations institutionalized ties to politicians and in consequence legitimated them. When citizens picked up a nineteenth-century newspaper, they knew what they were getting. In the twentieth century, the ideal of objectivity masked a solicitude that admitted few effective countervailing responses.

By the New Deal years, this sort of "cozy relationship between reporters and officials" extended to the press conference, according to James Reston, who never quite reconciled himself to the "bantering atmosphere of these clubby gatherings." Others seemed to entertain few qualms. A number of important White House correspondents in the Cold War period not only disavowed popular politics in favor of the professional ideology of democratic realism but also relieved their social anxieties in the process. Thus the legendary journalist Merriman Smith, noting that President Dwight D. Eisenhower refused to flatter the White House press corps with extra attention, could state without embarrassment that "reporters were justified when they deplored his lack of after-hours or social contact with them." (Jack Kennedy evidently made things right for Smith. "I felt Kennedy understood me," Smith recounted in his memoir.) Kennedy's charm turned newsmen such as Arthur Krock, Hugh Sidey, and Benjamin Bradlee from objective newsmen into sycophants. They were more likely to swim naked with the president in the White House pool—as Sidey did in his capacity as Washington correspondent for *Time* magazine—than to analyze Kennedy's behavior and its implications for American politics.

The nineteenth-century reporter, Ben: Perley Poore (sometimes, Benjamin: Perley Poore), and his colleagues on newspaper row never divulged everything they knew about the workings of government. Nor did efforts to discredit officials by circulating gossip meet unqualified approbation in the age of popular politics. In 1850, Jane Grey Swisshelm marked the beginning of her tenure as a Washington correspondent by printing allegations that Daniel Webster had sired two illegitimate mulatto children. "Webster was supposed to be a moral as well as an intellectual giant," yet "his life was full of rottenness," she later explained. Nevertheless, Horace Greeley, her boss, swiftly fired her. Swisshelm had no regrets; her story was "copied and copied," and Webster's reputation suffered. "Even Mr. Greeley continued to be my friend, and I wrote for the *Tribune* often after that time." Swisshelm and like-minded contemporaries could justify such actions by invoking the popular sentiment that animated democratic republicanism or evangelical Protestantism. Twentieth-century correspondents, by contrast, endorsed a more deliberate, clinical form of politics. As professionals infatuated with rationality, objectivity, and expertise, they identified with men in power and found themselves in need of the cooperation of their subjects, who set the terms of the arrangement.

Insulation augmented the authority of journalists as experts by conferring upon exposure an even more sensational cast. Popular books by reporters such as Clinton Wallace Gilbert, Drew Pearson, Robert Allen, Jack Lait, and Lee Mortimer vowed to deliver rumors stolen from behind the facades of officialdom. Reviewers praised Gilbert's *The Mirrors of Washington* (1921) for its "amusingly impertinent" evaluation of personal foibles. The book, snickered the *New York Times,* "contains indiscretions delicious enough to satisfy the most exacting." Reviews of *Washington Merry-Go-Round* (1931), coauthored by Pearson and Allen, similarly assured that "every gossipy or cynical soul will find its detail and its insouciant irreverence vastly amusing and entertaining." Yet neither Gilbert nor Pearson and Allen betrayed confidences by disclosing unsavory rumors about sexual immorality, though the latter excoriated the "smug sycophancy and the disgusting timidity of the majority of the correspondents and especially of the 'trained seal' group." In *Washington Confidential* (1951), reporters Jack Lait and Lee Mortimer testified to their willingness to announce sexual immorality among national politicians. "That's why we were born—to tell you what you couldn't find out without us—Confidential!" As promised, the pair proved more indiscreet than either Gilbert or the team of Pearson and Allen. They printed the names and addresses of Washington prostitutes, for instance, and such lines as: "A man of almost Cabinet rank in the Defense Department is also a pervert, with bivalent tendencies, a two-way performer." Nevertheless, their blunt discussion of transgressions by public officials eschewed full disclosure. "We will not divulge names, or tell how they cover up. Your imagination will picture how easy it is in a town where so many are seeking favors, to get a stooge to come along as the cutie's alleged 'date,' while the principal apparently came along only for the ride." Bearing seductive titles and employing clever marketing strategies—Gilbert, and Pearson and Allen initially published their books anonymously—these works traded on the idiom of exposure while manifesting an emerging class of Washington insiders privy to the hidden exertions of politicians. In time, the sort of measured gossip they peddled became institutionalized. Clinton Gilbert wrote a column for *Collier's* titled "The Man at the Keyhole." Merriman Smith's twice-weekly "Backstairs at the White House" ran in newspapers from the 1930s to the 1970s, while Drew Pearson and Robert Allen (and, later, Jack Anderson) published the most feared syndicated column in the nation for forty years. These men excelled in the delicate task of revealing just enough information to keep readers vaguely interested and politicians vaguely nervous.

Candidates and voters agreed that personal virtue remained important for asserting political authority in the twentieth century, then, but a professionalized journalism hostile to the perceived excesses of popular politics refused to divulge the embarrassing sexual practices of powerful officials. A by-product of journalism's paternalistic mood, insulation also proved an expedient means by which reporters could establish themselves as experts in a segmented, hierarchical society. Newspapermen entered the ranks of professional elites by subscribing to the prevailing tenet that political decision making required insulation from mob-like and irrational voters.

▮▮▮

This explanation for the return of reticence is vulnerable to at least two objections. First, unlike other areas of specialized inquiry, American journalism generally lacked formal internal disciplinary mechanisms. As a result, the field was never fully professionalized. What explains the restraint displayed by tabloid newspapermen such as Walter Winchell and by somewhat marginalized figures such as Pearson, Gilbert, Lait, and Mortimer? These men betrayed an uneasy relationship with the ethical codes of the ASNE.

Consider Winchell's reticence about the infidelities of New York City mayor Jimmy Walker, who pursued forbidden sexual pleasures throughout the 1920s, unafraid that a demand for accountability might lead to public opprobrium. Throughout his term, "the reporters tried to protect Jim from himself," according to the newsman Gene Fowler. Even Winchell—"the great revealer of other people's secrets," according to biographer Neal Gabler—knew about and suppressed news of the mayor's habits. Only after the beginning of the Seabury investigations, which revealed rampant corruption in his regime, did word of Walker's mistress filter into the tabloids.

A second, related objection to the focus on professional-class journalism concerns the motives of politicians themselves. What explains their reticence? Partisanship lost some of its fury in the twentieth century, but it hardly died. Surely disclosures of candidates' adulteries could have reaped political gain. Yet in 1920 Democrats possessed information about Harding's assignations and did not make use of it. Republicans possessed legal papers in 1960 concerning an illegitimate child allegedly fathered by John Kennedy but declined to divulge the matter in public. Whatever their disagreements, leaders in the major parties entered the century determined to temper open discussions about sexual indiscretion and related topics. In 1880, the House of Representatives adopted Rule XIV, which instructed a floor speaker to "confine himself to the question under debate, avoiding personality." Two decades later, California legislators passed a sweeping, short-lived statute that made illegal the publication of "any caricature of any person residing in this state, which caricature will in any manner reflect upon the honor, integrity, manhood, virtue, reputation, or business or political motives of the person so caricatured, or which tends to expose the individual so caricatured to public hatred, ridicule, or contempt." Other state assemblies—including New York's in 1897, Indiana's in 1913, and Alabama's in 1915—attempted similar proscriptions of nineteenth-century methods of politicking. A Pennsylvania initiative in 1903 lambasted "evil gossip" and "groundless rumors" and outlawed any newspaper story "affecting the character, reputation or business of citizens."

The transformation of journalism is, at best, an incomplete explanation for the return of reticence. The other part of the explanation concerns the political psychology of national state building. During the tumultuous decades after the 1880s, the relatively weak, attenuated structures of nineteenth-century government power faced myriad threats: intensifying class divisions, reckless corporate power, menacing domestic radicals and international enemies, and an increasingly disorderly, complex society. A broad group of reformers that included Mugwumps, Progressives, and, later, New Dealers responded to these crises by building "an entirely new framework for governmental operations," according to political scientist Stephen Skowronek. In place of the local controls and party "bossism" that characterized much of nineteenth-century government emerged a centralized administrative bureaucracy comprising an expanded federal judiciary and regulatory agencies. This reconstructed state confronted the challenges of industrial capitalism by concentrating power in hierarchical offices staffed by managers, specialists, and other elites. This panoramic nationalization of governmental power—which also called forth a muscular chief executive—generated a "sense of the state" famously absent from American political life in the Nineteenth Century.

In a democratic republic whose citizens still harbored suspicions of concentrated power, that sense of the state demanded cultural as well as legal justification. Transforming elitist ideas about power into legitimate authority demanded a new cultural frame through which Americans could see the federal government. Reticence about sex contributed to this frame by bestowing prestige upon politicians. To say that politicians circulated new status claims is not to say that those claims were always and everywhere honored. Nor does it imply that their status pretensions were necessarily proportionate to the actual structure of the national government. The burden of the argument here is to suggest why those with access to the means of mass communication abandoned one public gesture for another, more constricted one. The ideological function of prestige helps explain the change.

Preserving the moral integrity of twentieth-century political elites unified the nation around the federal state. Reticence implied that between the polity and the state lay a symbolic distance. Political authority appeared not immediate and corporeal, but abstract and intangible, shrouded in *the office* of the presidency and other protected images that together functioned as a bulwark against dissent. This, at least, was the hope of Herbert Croly and other evangelists of "American national integrity." Croly disliked "rowdy journalism" for its "abusive attacks" and looked forward to "a completer mutual confidence between a few exceptional leaders and the many plain people," as he wrote in his influential treatise, *The Promise of American Life.* "We ought to know," continued Croly, remarking on invective as a kind of public rhetoric, "that the prejudices and passions provoked by language of this kind violate the essential principle of both nationality and democracy." As Croly said, his ideas about democratic procedures fitted well within the Hamiltonian tradition that nineteenth-century popular politics had swept aside. "Anything which undermines executive authority in this country seriously threatens our national integrity and balance," Croly wrote. The 1903 Pennsylvania initiative against "evil gossip" even more clearly connected attacks on the personal morality of individual politicians with the legitimacy of federal authority. "A whole generation of young men are being trained to a familiarity with crime and to disrespect for government," complained the bill's sponsor, who then articulated the sentiment that lay behind Croly's remarks. "It is not the individual attacked who is alone concerned. The Commonwealth is interested that those who render her service should be treated with deference and respect, so that when they go forth in the performance of her functions those to whom they are sent may feel that they are vested with authority."

Reactions to the posthumous Harding revelations indicated the growing importance of reticence to national authority. In Philadelphia, a local attorney filed an injunction to halt stage productions of Samuel Hopkins Adams's book *Revelry,* which portrayed Harding's immoralities, on the sole ground that Adams "flaunts the Federal Government and ridicules high officials." The theater owner chased the play out of the city, calling the production "essentially unpatriotic." Congressman John Tillman, denouncing Nan Britton's book on the floor of the House of Representatives, insisted that suppressing news of presidential adultery constituted "a matter of nation-wide interest and importance. It is a non-partisan question." Richard Washburn Child, the diplomat, onetime editor of *Collier's,* and former ambassador to Italy who collaborated with Benito Mussolini on the latter's autobiography, proposed "Commandment no. 11: Thou shalt not whisper falsely against thy President." Writing in *Collier's,* Child maintained that "American citizenship owes it to [presidents and other statesman] to reject the word-of-mouth story and the whispered slander." Explaining the reluctance of media figures to discuss any of Harding's trespasses, another reviewer upheld the argument that "the majority feel . . . that it is not only beneath their dignity but a breach of their patriotic integrity to notice such terrible statements about a dead ex-President of the United States and other officials high in the honored (or dishonored?) places of government." Appeals to the dignity, power, and honor of the national government and its chief representatives did not present themselves so easily in the Nineteenth Century.

Subsequent to the 1920s a series of crises—the Great Depression, World War II, the Cold War—vastly strengthened those appeals. Thus C. Wright Mills witnessed a "penumbra of prestige" shadowing postwar American leaders, who successfully perpetuated and consolidated the "nationalization of status" undertaken by their forebears. In fact, by the time that Mills blasted the "power elite" and Kennedy readied himself to lead it, everyone who held a position in the national firmament—from tabloid journalists to major publishers to partisan officials themselves—had learned to operate according to a tacit understanding guided by a political psychology: exposing certain personal vices of presidents imperiled the legitimacy of the state's claim to concentrated power. Within a political culture that still expected leaders to obey community standards of virtue, immunity from moral scrutiny was a critical weapon of the Cold War. During this period most political news became national news, and all national news became foreign and thus potentially hostile news. Journalists who reported what they knew about John Kennedy's adultery, for instance, would risk not simply fewer of those White House swimming parties but allegations of disloyalty.

The mutually reinforcing relationship between legitimating elite power and insulating moral turpitude explains why the allegations about Jimmy Walker and Warren Harding could circulate *after* their administrations had fallen into disrepute. Once their public authority had been called into question, the task of keeping their personal transgressions secret made sense only to their most vigorous protectors. This connection also illuminates the uneven application of privacy by journalists. Reporters who covered private ceremonies such as Alice Roosevelt's 1906 wedding did not undercut the authority of an incipient power elite; such events rarely involved serious moral infractions. Nor did the scrutiny directed at celebrities in the first half of the century matter in this context. The cultural vestments required by hierarchical political power were absent—and irrelevant.

███

From the 1790s through the 1890s, attacks on sexual character underscored the democratic republicanism and evangelical Protestantism that dominated the period's public life. In the eight decades that followed the Cleveland-Halpin scandal, candidates continued to present themselves as men of good sexual character, yet official political culture no longer regarded them—in the phrase the English traveler Wortley used in 1851—as "the most atrocious criminals," who inevitably harbored shameful secrets about sex. Reticence and insulation dislodged gossip and exposure from political communication.

Recently, as journalism has de-professionalized and as the federal government has retreated, sex scandals have returned to the foreground of our political life. Many liberals deplore the return, since liberalism repudiates both the civic virtue associated with democratic republicanism and the public morality entailed by evangelicalism. Still, these alternative political traditions hold the loyalty of citizens. The commercialism of the tabloid press cheapens the core concern of these traditions—how to ensure responsible governance—but they deserve respect nonetheless, not least because politicians routinely *invite* attention to favorable features of their ostensibly personal lives, wishing, like other celebrities, to have it both ways as they create, manipulate, and peddle their images in pursuit of the seats of power.

Then again, privacy is not the same as secrecy, and salutary efforts to achieve transparency in government should take care to respect the former while denouncing the latter. Keeping irresponsible power at bay requires sustained and intense scrutiny of officials, but failing to uphold their individual legal rights would rob such publicity of its moral force.

In my view, the most important criterion to consider is whether sex scandals inhibit or promote the free flow of political discussion. The same assumptions and developments that drove scandal from the optic of political culture after the 1890s—the decline of political parties and the rise of an ostensibly autonomous journalism, the advent of a version of democratic thought that prized political engineering over political participation, and the construction of nationalized state apparatus—introduced a sense of enervation and desiccation into the twentieth-century polity. As the scope and reach of the federal government enlarged and lengthened, the number and nature of secrets reposed within it also grew, sexual transgressions among them. Organized, effective dissent declined. C. Wright Mills wrote in 1952: "Increasingly we feel that there is something synthetic about our big men. Their style, and the conditions under which they became 'big,' opens them to the charge of the build-up and the front. One feels, even when it is not there, the slickness of the pre-fabricated. And, in fact, the advertising and public relations technique has been extended from the peddling of brand-name tooth paste and movie stars to the 'development' of national politicians."

The limited franchise meant that nineteenth-century popular politics was not a substantive democracy. The raucous public exchanges of that era did not always produce the deliberation or openness that a strong democracy demands. Too much salacious material, moreover, blunts the very sensibilities and capacities required for self-government. Nonetheless, the liberty to gossip in public about political leaders implies a breadth of freedom of expression that we should not voluntarily abrogate.

PITY WARREN HARDING

To the Editor:

It is a saddening thing when the labors of a graduate department (the University of Rochester), three editors of this *Journal,* and several anonymous readers designated by the *Journal* fail to protect a graduate student, as happened, we believe, with the lead article in the issue for December 2000. The author of the article has a bright future, as this academic year he is teaching at Harvard. He writes well, and it would not surprise us if the piquant subject of his article, "What Happened to Sex Scandals: Politics and Peccadilloes, Jefferson to Kennedy," might gain him a New York or Boston contract. Unfortunately the array of editorial talent offered this author has failed to protect him from a basic error: it is wrong, downright wrong, for a historian to assert what he or she cannot prove. Perhaps a journalist, in the heat of a deadline, might be excused for failing to get in touch with a historian who knows the subject—journalists never read anything if they can telephone some "source." But for a historian, no.

The author of the article in question asserts flatly that Nan Britton was the mistress of President Warren G. Harding and that Lucy Mercer Rutherfurd (the name is misspelled in the article) and Marguerite LeHand were mistresses of President Franklin D. Roosevelt. How can he possibly prove those assertions?

Consider first his accusation—it is in reality a character assassination and one of his academic readers should have caught it—about President Harding. Admittedly one of the undersigned is the author of a book defending the president, published five years ago, which contains an entire chapter on Britton. No writer likes to learn that his book is "unpersuasive." But the book goes far beyond the two serious sources mentioned by the *Journal's* author (the others are Henry L. Mencken and Dorothy Parker), that is, the sixty-two-year-old diatribe by the muckraker Samuel Hopkins Adams and the biography by the Harding hater Francis Russell. Have the *Journal's* editors heard of the federal court case with the amusing title, *Britton v. Klunk* (1931), tried in Toledo, in which Britton brought suit against a Marion hotel keeper who sold a book in his hotel lobby that was hostile to her own book published several years before? She asked $50,000 damages. She rested her case on the unsupported statements in her own book. At the end of the proceedings her attorney reduced her demand for damages to one cent, the jury debated an hour, and refused the cent. In subsequent years nothing, absolutely nothing, has appeared to support her book. Britton's papers opened a year ago in the UCLA library and there is no smoking gun. A presidential historian, Glen Abel of Los Angeles, interviewed Britton's daughter, Elizabeth Ann Blaesing, who would say only that all her mother had to say was in the papers.

The Roosevelt accusations are equally indefensible. It is true that the Roosevelt family was appalled by the revelation in 1966 by the journalist Jonathan Daniels of the friendship between the president and Mrs. Rutherfurd. One of the saddest exchanges it is possible to read is in the papers of the president's daughter Anna at the Roosevelt Library in Hyde Park, in which she pleaded with Daniels not to publish anything from the former Lucy Mercer, a plea that Daniels refused in the name of history. But the point here is that neither of the principals, the president or Mrs. Rutherfurd, testified about this issue. It therefore lies in the realm of uncertainty: no historian should claim that it happened. Same for the president's secretary, Marguerite LeHand.

We call attention of *Journal* readers to the fact that in the same issue in which the article appears is a brilliant article by Howard Jones showing how a novelist and several historians accused the leader of the *Amistad* rebellion in the mid-nineteenth century, Cin-qué, of engaging in the slave trade once he returned to Africa. As Jones writes in enlightening detail, there is not a scintilla of proof of this. The *Journal* properly sponsored the refutation.

Robert H. Ferrell
Indiana University
Bloomington, Indiana

Warren G. Harding III
Cincinnati, Ohio

To the Editor:

My statements concerning sexual affairs by Warren G. Harding and Franklin D. Roosevelt are incidental to the conceptual concerns of the article. I could have written "alleged" and produced the same argument. This point seems lost on Warren G. Harding III and Robert Ferrell, who, as defenders of President Harding, show little interest in the arguments of my article. Still, I did assert that Harding and Roosevelt each had sexual liaisons, and I am happy to accept responsibility for these claims.

Surely, most readers of this journal understand why standards of "proof" for sexual intercourse, unlike slave trading, frequently retreat to the circumstantial. Nonetheless, creditable warrants for these scandals exist. As far as I know, no scholar has disputed the work of Jonathan Daniels and Joseph P. Lash. According to Lash's interview with her daughter, Eleanor Roosevelt herself knew of the Mercer affair. The foregoing letter adds nothing to this historiography except indignation. I have nothing to add except an item in the Private Papers of Drew Pearson (duly cited), which states that few of the principals in Washington's insider culture long remained unaware of the president's activities. It is a settled matter, though many of the private details concerning Mercer and especially Missy LeHand will necessarily remain obscure or absent from the historical record.

As for Harding, Nan Britton's own testimony in *The President's Daughter* persuaded me, in part because biographer Francis Russell discovered in 1963 a large cache of love letters written from President Harding to Carrie F. Phillips, about whom Ferrell and Harding III are silent. The cache of letters proved beyond doubt the Harding-Phillips affair and lent credibility to Britton's own claims. According to Russell, Britton's detailed description of the letters that Harding wrote to her, which she claimed to have destroyed upon his request, closely matched the Phillips letters.

Why the authors parade *Britton v. Klunk* before the *Journal's* readers is puzzling. Britton was the plaintiff, not the defendant, and she sued for libel in a case adjudicated in Ohio only five months after President Calvin Coolidge arrived in Marion to dedicate the Harding Memorial. Robert Ferrell's own description of the proceedings shows overwhelming judicial bias against Britton. The judge, moreover, permitted no newspaper reporters in the courtroom for most of the trial, and the official records of the case have been lost. What the proceedings in this trial showed or failed to show, therefore, clearly rests within a "realm of uncertainty." On page 71 of his book, Robert Ferrell writes this about the case: "It is not possible to discover much about what happened." In the end, I found his interpretation of the Britton-Harding relationship riddled with unpersuasive speculation and his approach lacking in fair regard for both sides.

Not much has surfaced to support Britton's claims. Nor has much surfaced to refute them. Absent a "smoking gun" (perhaps "blue dress" is now a better metaphor) the history of sex scandals will remain matters for creditable warrants, and thus for careful reconstruction.

In my view, the dearth of affirmative material underscores the achievements of reticence as a political psychology and an aim of official power that seeks to consecrate itself with moral authority. The history of the Harding-Britton relationship is littered with examples of heavy-handed behavior. With help from the New York City police department, the publishing plates for *The President's Daughter* initially were seized, her office invaded, and her reputation smeared by John S. Sumner and the New York Society for the Suppression of Vice. An assistant United States attorney opened an "investigation" of her. First Lady Florence Harding destroyed an undetermined number of her husband's private papers only weeks after his death. Despite requests by the Library of Congress, the Harding Memorial Association denied access to many of the remaining papers for more than four decades, a willful obstruction of free discussion.

For his retelling of the Harding-Britton relationship long after it had been exposed and discussed in the 1920s, Francis Russell was sued by Warren Harding III. Few historians would be pleased with the terms of the settlement, which placed the most important evidence for Harding's personal life, his adulterous letters to Carrie F. Phillips, under lock-and-key in the Library of Congress until July 29, 2014. Does Warren Harding III wish to help revise these terms, and allow this matter the chance to move toward the realm of certainty?

Twentieth-century journalists and others grew more reticent about sex scandals partially as a response to the union of intellect and political power, of the kind in evidence in this patronizing letter. We ought to resist such attempts to prop up the glory of the American presidency. Unnecessary secrets weaken popular government. And no president should fail to understand that the office is not a private fiefdom. Only when elected officials stop fleeing the judgment of the people over whom they presume to rule can that judgment hope to prove itself worthy of the high ideals of American democracy.

John H. Summers
University of Rochester
Rochester, New York

THE SAN FRANCISCO LEFT

City Lights Bookstore slopes against a hill, then bends with the street around a sharp curve. Like many establishments in San Francisco, its appearance changes dramatically in relation to one's angle of vision. Here, however, the message is the same from every direction. From the front window on the second floor, a hand-painted sign looks out over the street: "Depose Bush and Cheney." Inside, shelves carry labels such as "Class War" and "Stolen Continents." A brochure sums up the animating idea: "City Lights is one of the few truly great independent bookstores in the United States—a place where book lovers from across the country and around the world come to browse, read, and just soak in the ambience of alternative culture's only Literary Landmark."

North Beach, the neighborhood surrounding The Landmark, is littered with upmarket bistros and bars. Strip clubs jut into the sidewalks with gaudy neon signs: "Garden of Eden, Taste our Forbidden Fruit." City Lights neither stands *independent* of these blights nor presents any *alternative* aesthetic. From the strip club signs it borrows hyperbole; from the bistros it takes its retail sheen. The Landmark is a symbol of the postwar avant-garde's failed effort to transcend the moralism of high culture and the banality of mass culture. Not for nothing did it end up a stop on the tour bus.

As I passed through the entrance and took the brochure, the woman minding the register brought me up short, telling me to deposit my belongings behind her counter. Annoyed, I began to reply with a sarcastic comment about preemption. Then I noticed how she wore the same etiolated mask as every other retail clerk I had encountered, and I acquiesced.

▮▮▮

I founded my decision to spend a month in San Francisco on a set of associations and tendencies, and some knowledge, concerning the city's reputation for radical politics and literature. I wanted to see for myself. Back in New England, politics emanates from the engineering ethos of academic technicians and from the sedate, educative style inherited from Progressive reformers. Here, the quality of politics was different.

As soon as I arrived in the city, in July 2004, I saw street signs boldly commemorating the 70th anniversary of the San Francisco General Strike. Longshoremen had closed the ports for two months, bringing the city to a standstill in the middle of the Depression and drawing 130,000 workers out with them. Congress, worried that strike would grow into an insurrection, had passed social welfare legislation historians call "the second New Deal."

In political terms, 70 years might as well be 700, but on this night Alexander Cockburn and Jeffrey St. Clair, co-editors of the muckraking journal *Counterpunch*, were scheduled to speak on the second floor of City Lights. Their topic was the upcoming presidential contest between George Bush and John Kerry, which was billed by the press as "the most important election in decades."

Cockburn's car had broken down, we learned at the outset. St. Clair would have the floor to himself. From his first remarks it was apparent that he intended to make a case against President Bush without making the corresponding case for candidate Kerry. St. Clair accused the parties of colluding to reduce political competition at the district level. On issues such as drugs, oil, and poverty, he went on, not a "dime's worth of difference" separated them. He departed slightly from the logic of equivalence when he evinced special contempt for one of the men, challenging the audience "to name a single virtuous thing about John Kerry's character." A woman called our attention to Kerry's opposition to the Vietnam War. St. Clair countered that Kerry had arranged his antiwar statements in accordance with his political aspirations. St. Clair seemed to be saying that as soon as Kerry's virtue mixed with his politics,

it became a vice. This was confusing. He had condemned President
Bush for refusing to submit his ideas to political debate; now he
condemned Kerry for the opposite reason. Then St. Clair said he
"favored anything disruptive to the social order." Before anybody
had a chance to ask whether he meant to endorse the attacks of
September 11, he said he believed the World Trade Center had offered "a legitimate target."

Of the 30 members of the audience, half seemed to be talking
at once, not talking so much as hissing and jeering. "This is for all
you *so-called* radicals," began one outburst. Another man, sitting
directly behind me, asked, "Do you believe the Israeli security
service plotted 9/11 in secret, or do you believe the government's
story, the story the *New York Times* tries to tell us?" St. Clair said
nothing in response.

▌▌▌

Disappointing though the speech was, it did not shake my belief in
the underlying truth of the analysis. St. Clair was right. The most
important division in American politics was not between Republicans and Democrats and their candidates. It was between those
who believe and participate in party politics and those who do not.
And those who believed in party politics were riveted, just then, to
the dueling conventions, where the party out of power supposed the
party in power to be the sole and exclusive author of present trouble.
Why had Democrats failed to protect organized labor? *Why* had they
failed to come up with any distinctive foreign policy ideas in the
last thirty years? Such questions appeared inconvenient, irritating,
or intelligible strictly in terms of the character and strength of the
opposition, as if the character and strength of the opposition were
a fixed variable. A third party was trying to emerge to address such
questions, and in due time both the third party and its candidates
were put down as impracticable and therefore as irresponsible in-
terlopers in the business at hand.

Most Americans view the two parties as little more than mobile
battalions of money, whereas most political intellectuals tend to see
them as they see themselves, representatives of rival philosophies

locked in combat. One can only marvel at the willingness of each generation of professors, pundits, and foundation publicists to embrace labels that long ago ceased to explain anything meaningful. Two world wars exhausted the nineteenth-century division of political philosophy into liberals and conservatives. Yet contemporary discussion is dominated by "neo-liberals" and "neo-conservatives." What is next? Neo-neo-liberals and neo-neo-conservatives? (And then?) Bereft of a coherent ideology by which to measure political reality, liberals and leftists have struggled mightily to assimilate the most obvious facts. In their confusion at the sight of a supposedly anti-government party prosecuting a federal drug war, in their outrage at the sight of a supposedly pro-government party prosecuting welfare recipients, they overlook that the targets of these policies are often the same people.

■■■

The malign consequences of the party duopoly are easiest to see among those who interpret democratic politics not merely as a set of procedures and policies, but also as a social system that seeks to elevate the moral quality of life. What can be done? Several days after visiting City Lights, I went to see Chris Carlsson, cofounder and presiding editor of *Processed World*. The magazine was started in the eighties by pissed-off, yuppie-hating office workers in the Financial District. *Processed World* was as intelligent as *democracy*, its East-Coast equivalent, and much funnier. Unfortunately, the circle of writers, activists and office workers around *Processed World* found that it could not translate cultural protest against the machinery of the information age into effective political action.

Chris invited me to a board meeting in the magazine's downtown office, where I observed a cadre of burned-out contributors and editors swill beer, smoke pot, and mouth anti-capitalist slogans. Chris handed me a leaflet he had written, which had been circulating all summer in the city's anti-war movement: "We are bound up in a collective madness, a mass psychosis, that is shaped daily by a media wildly out of touch with reality. We knew perfectly well what was going to happen, and sadly, we were right. Nearly everything predicted by the anti-war movement has come to pass, and it just gets worse with each passing day." Sad, indeed. After the meeting, Chris volunteered a thought that perfectly reproduced the vitiating mix of aggression and complacency in the leaflet. "I would not be too upset if one of these people were assassinated," he said of the Bush cabinet.

Anti-Bush feeling was intense at this moment, and not only in San Francisco. Soon after Chris made his private remark, Nicholson Baker raised the question of assassination publicly in *Checkpoint*. The novel consists of a debate between two friends, Jay and Ben, on the problem posed by the Bush junta. Ben seeks to dissuade Jay from carrying through his assassination plans; but not because he thinks Bush deserves to live, only because the bad consequences would outweigh the good.

These examples should answer J.M. Coetzee, who asks in *Diary of a Bad Year* how Americans can tolerate the condition of disgrace into which the administration has plunged them. "Impossible to believe that in some American hearts the spectacle of their country's honor being dragged through the mud does not breed murderous thoughts. Impossible to believe that no one has yet plotted to assassinate these criminals in high office."

███

Coetzee himself subscribes to a politics of "pessimistic anarchistic quietism, or anarchist quietistic pessimism, or pessimistic quietistic anarchism." He thinks of himself as an anarchist "because experience tells me that what is wrong with politics is power itself." Anarchism, so understood, has flourished in San Francisco, where many people consider the government in Washington DC almost as a foreign power and so have refused to obey its equation of law and morality. This refusal, however, has made it difficult to master the political metaphysics of disgrace. How can one assert the libertarian or anarchist perspective if it is, by definition, outside the law?

The radicals I encountered, unable to overcome the paradox, were distant both from the party system and from the people in whose name they spoke. Conservatism had begun in the twenties and thirties in a similar predicament, as a moral reaction against the abstract and impersonal qualities of mass society. Fundamentalism and neo-evangelicalism succeeded when their leaders recreated in religious symbols the modes of trust, interaction, and sacrifice that once characterized their small communities. Without such projects of revaluation and recommunalization, discontent fades from negativism or spins illusions of omnipotence.

Coetzee chooses "willed obscurity, inner emigration" as the third way between servitude and revolt. A radical political intelligence that expects to succeed must eventually move past sorrow and grievance and envision ideas and projects. On my last night in the city I encountered the absence of such imagination, this painful isolation of the San Francisco left, when I attended an "educational forum" about Cuba, sponsored by the radical group ANSWER.

■■■

Somewhere between 100 and 150 people attended the forum. Those who could not find chairs sat in the aisles, or filed along the walls underneath banners that read "Free the Cuban 5!" (a reference to five Cuban spies imprisoned in the United States since 2001) or leaned against tables stacked with t-shirts, buttons, pamphlets, petitions, and magazines. In opening remarks the chairman urged us to avail ourselves of the instructional material and expressed his hope that the knowledge so gained would be put to use in "direct action." The restlessness of the audience, its palpable sense of purpose, and the location—we were gathered in The Mission, the impoverished Hispanic district of the city—caused the room to fill up with the desperate energy of a revival meeting.

The best speaker that evening, a woman named Carol Cross, reported that her group recently had entered Cuba illegally from Mexico. When the group had tried to return from Cuba to Mexico, agents from the Border Patrol, Homeland Security, and Treasury swarmed them. All eighty people had been ordered from the bus, searched, and photographed. Ms. Cross compared their "refusal to be intimidated" to the spirit of the freedom riders in the civil rights movement. "There's a higher law, and we're just not going to pay attention to these petty laws," she said.

How little insight they gained by their sacrifice! Although the four speakers had visited the island at differing times, with differing organizations, for differing reasons, they appeared to have seen the same things and indeed to have come to the same conclusion. Cuba, they agreed, had no poverty, no violent crime, no illiteracy, no drug trafficking, no police brutality, no racism, no human rights abuses, no dissidents. Children played in the streets after dark without fear. Hospitals ministered to the sick with skill and alacrity. Universities spread sweetness and light.

On these points the four spoke in unison. One of the speakers raised the idea that Fidel Castro was a dictator, only to put the idea down as calculated misinformation. "I mean, it is mind boggling, the propaganda. How can a whole people be suppressed for 45 years without a major upheaval?" The people of Castro's "so-called regime" had asked him to deliver a message to Americans: "They want you to know they are ready to die for the revolution." He delivered the message without a trace of irony.

The final speaker adopted the same rhetoric of extenuation. Yes, she said, there have been state executions of malcontents, and yes, she did oppose the death penalty, especially as it is applied to political crimes. But these malcontents had tried to subvert Cuba at the bidding of the United States government, a declared enemy. To refuse to punish them was to abdicate national sovereignty. She finished her speech with a call for a political revolution in the United States.

To this the crowd responded with whistles, cheers, and waves of applause. Nobody asked any questions.

A NOTE ON
ANTI-AMERICANISM

Czeslaw Milosz used "political correctness" to describe the collapse of metaphysical and political levels of argument into a singular "New Faith." This fusion seems to be going on in American intellectual circles. I refer to the multiplying uses of the phrase, anti-American.

To be anti-American seems to mean to violate decency, to do violence to an absolute truth. Understood in this way, the phrase realigns the conventional left-right groupings in the United States around the axis of state power. Thus does Norman Podhoretz range liberal internationalists, Republican realists, and the "anti-American left" into de-facto allies merely because each group doubts the wisdom of the Iraq occupation.

Podhoretz views modern American history as a succession of noble wars, a view that has the advantage of simplifying things into good and evil, winners and defeatists, patriots and subversives, free societies and "swamps" that must be "drained." Since violence, in his view, is the instrument of historical change, diversity of opinion is the main threat. "Facing a conflict that may well go on for three or four decades," Podhoretz writes in his book, *World War IV*, "Americans of this generation are called upon to be more patient than 'the greatest generation' needed to be in World War II, which for us lasted only four years; and facing an enemy even more elusive than the Communists, the American people of today are required to summon at least as much perseverance as the American people of those days did—for all their bitching and moaning—over the 47 long years of World War III."

Why morale should be so important to a war that is so manifest-ly just and necessary Podhoretz never quite explains. Milosz would have recognized the cast of his thought. In contrast to republican and democratic thinkers, who usually do not consecrate political authority, Podhoretz conflates the practical necessities of national security with the preservation of the national honor. This confla-tion, so common in conservative political thought, discourages the analysis of institutions in favor of the flattery of a charismatic leader. Podhoretz writes of "the amazing leader this President has amazingly turned out to be." He praises President Bush for his heart, stomach, and will, all the military virtues. Intelligence is tasked with moral surveillance of the many-sided opposition.

Those who are still willing to think freely about such matters might recall the old distinctions between country, government, and state. As Randolph Bourne wrote, the idea of country comprises the social and cultural life of the people. It bears the common memories, habits, and values which make an American different from a Canadian, and an Englishman different from an Irishman. The idea of country embraces these differences without rancor or rivalry. The government is the practical machinery by which the country conceives, debates, and agrees upon its laws. It comprises the temporary administrations, parliaments or coalitions. The state constitutes the apparatus of coercion, the monopoly of the means of violence. It collects the taxes, polices the territory, makes the wars.

On the strength of these distinctions we can reply to those who use "anti-American" as a slogan of abuse and intimidation that they mix up attitudes toward country and nation with attitudes toward state. They make themselves deputies in the state's campaign of propaganda against its citizens. This in itself is no surprise. As consumers turn themselves into salespeople for the corporations that jilt them, so do the state's most fanatical agents emerge from the formally free institutions of the country.

What is surprising is that contemporary elites have abandoned the vocabulary of obligation. Talk of national duty once eased the transformation of the free intellectual, who owed the highest obligation to culture itself, to the political ideologist willing to obfuscate for the sake of ends over which he exerted little direct control. Today the state does not even have to ask for such blind allegiance, though news from American journalism indicates that it is willing to pay cash for it, and there are buyers aplenty.

Reviving a link between popular sovereignty and mental freedom means refusing to be intimidated by allegations of anti-Americanism, and, equally so, refusing to be baited by the division of intellectuals into "soft" and "hard" with respect to state enemies. It is worth remembering how long this distinction has poisoned debate. Waldo Frank and Lewis Mumford used it to knock around John Dewey's pragmatism in *The New Republic* in the late 1930s. Frank and Mumford charged then that pragmatic attitudes weakened the capacity to recognize the threat of European fascism. Their caricatures helped put two generations of liberal opinion on war footing, and drove Dewey into gloomy forecasting. "It is quite conceivable that after the next war we should have in this country a semi-military, semi-financial autocracy, which would fasten class divisions on this country for untold years," Dewey wrote in 1939. "In any case we should have the suppression of all the democratic values for the sake of which we professedly went to war."

Dewey's mood recovered, but his influence did not. The attacks of the late 1930s helped kill off the moral and political relevance of radical democratic thought for twenty years. By the 1950s the landscape of moral argument about foreign policy lay barren. Reviewing the work of Reinhold Niebuhr and Walter Lippmann in 1957, the philosopher Morton White complained, "It seems to me a sad commentary on the social thought of today that two of the most popular social thinkers on the American scene can produce nothing more original than the doctrines of original sin and natural law as answers to the pressing problems of this age."

The attacks on pragmatism in the late 1930s, the attacks on New Leftists in the 1960s, and the attacks on "relativists" and "postmodernists" by liberal magazines in the weeks and months after September 11 betray a common anxiety. What they share is panic in the presence of free thought, as indicated by the notion that trying to understand a mass murder is tantamount to excusing or apologizing for it. Let us hope that we can move beyond a discussion in which one party continually rediscovers the loss of the republic, while the other continually rediscovers the birth of the empire. All parties may soon discover that they have no clue.

IN DREAMS BEGIN POLITICS

In *The Epic of America* (1931), the historian James Truslow Adams argued what many Americans have felt all along, that "there has been the *American dream*, that dream of a land in which life should be better and richer and fuller for every man, with opportunity for each according to his ability or achievement."

The campaign season, a prolonged divination of suppressed wishes, is prime-time for the rhetoric of the American Dream. But rhetoric is not the same as propaganda, and dreaming is more than a metaphor. Do politicians use their actual dreams as sources of innovation? What might their beliefs about dreaming imply about their style of decision-making? "She doesn't always know what to make of me," Barack Obama writes of his wife Michelle in *Dreams from My Father*. "She worries that, like Gramps and the Old Man, I am something of a dreamer." The autobiography mentions dreams on 38 occasions (once every 12 pages). It recounts Obama's own dreams as well as those of his friends and family, returning again and again to dreaming as a source of personal power and transcendence.

Raised in Hawaii and Indonesia, educated in Muslim and Catholic schools, Obama early on grew aware of the world of signs and symbols. References to evil spirits, exorcisms, demons, specters, totems, ghosts, and spells lie casually about the autobiography, which attests to his fascination with shrunken heads and "night runners" of Kenyan legend. The Republicans, in their restless nativism, have begun to use this part of Obama's biography to paint him as a foreigner. In truth, his sensitivity to unconscious and invisible forces makes him a fitting heir to a political unconscious that lies in the very bosom of the American past.

Cotton Mather is best remembered for *The Wonders of the Invisible World* and its argument for "Spectral Evidence" in the Salem witch trials. But his masterpiece was the *Magnalia Christi Americana, or, The Ecclesiastical History of New-England From Its First Planting, in the Year 1620, Unto the Year of Our Lord 1698,* the title indicating the mix of credulity and pedantry, the long passages of Greek that sat alongside reports of giant cows and visions of ships floating in the air. The most interesting of the *Magnalia*'s seven books consisted of biographies of the New England oligarchy, to whom Mather attributed a lively dream-life. He told how the early church fathers had asked his grandfather, John Cotton, to nominate a successor. Cotton was nearing death. One night a "fever dream" put into his mind the image of "Mr. Norton of Ipswich" riding into Boston on a white horse. The next morning Mr. Cotton nominated Mr. Norton in fact.

Mather's political equivalent in Virginia, William Byrd of Westover, recorded in his diary snatches of an enchanted world that belied his poise as prosperous statesman, scholar of science, and member of the political elite. One night in December 1710, Byrd dreamed of a flaming sword shooting across the sky. About a week later he was returning home from a walk with his wife. As they approached they saw the sword hanging in a cloud-bank over his house. "Both these appearances seemed to foretell some misfortune to me which afterwards came to pass in the death of several of my negroes after a very unusual manner," Byrd worried to his diary, adding this: "My wife about two months since dreamed she saw an angel in the shape of a big woman who told her that time was altered and the seasons were changed and that several calamities would follow that confusion. God avert his judgment from this poor country."

Leading thinkers of the revolutionary generation understood that putting the political affairs of the nation on a more rational basis entailed an attack on their metaphysics of dreaming. Benjamin Rush moved toward a scientific explanation in *Medical Inquiries* (1812), though his letters bared the ambivalence that dogged such moves. Writing to John Adams about a dream he had, in which Adams and

Thomas Jefferson ended their long estrangement, Rush brought about the reconciliation in fact.

A more potent attack came from Tom Paine, who published "Dream" in 1795 and later incorporated it into Part II of *The Age of Reason.* The stories of Ezekiel and Daniel, Paine pointed out, were narratives of captivity told from the point of view of prisoners of war. "They pretended to have dreamed dreams and seen visions, because it was unsafe for them to speak facts or plain language." To insist that God used dreams as a method of revelation was to abridge freedom of conscience, and freedom of conscience was a primary condition of freely fought politics.

███

The rise of America to a modern power-state elicited numberless comparisons to Rome without generating any literary equivalent to *Lives of the Caesars,* by the Roman biographer and dream-teller Suetonius. Caesar's last dream (according to Suetonius) sent him tumbling helplessly through space, soaring into the mouth of an abyss until, for one precious moment, he managed to touch the tip of Jupiter's finger. Lincoln's dreams were morbid by comparison. In his second term, the president suffered a nightmare at the start of which he became aware of the sound of weeping. He climbed out of his bed (in his dream) and went downstairs to the East Room. There he encountered a group of soldiers guarding a corpse. "Who is dead in the White House?' I demanded of one of the soldiers. 'The President,' was his answer; 'he was killed by an assassin!' Then came a loud burst of grief from the crowd, which awoke me from my dream."

Nor would Suetonius have overlooked Madame Marcia in her Dupont Circle parlor in the 1910s and 1920s. Marcia bought the latest editions of *Congressional Directory,* which she mined for astrologically important birth dates, though her best clients were the First Ladies. The most powerful women of the era, Edith Wilson and Florence Harding, each invited Marcia into the White House for secret horoscope readings. Florence Harding was an occultist whose belief in clairvoyance outdid even the fawning credulity in which Nancy Reagan beheld Joan Quigley. Mrs. Reagan, who has never asked forgiveness for ceding power to Ms. Quigley, has said in extenuation that the Hollywood dream-factory from which she and her husband came to politics was riddled by superstition. Just so.

"Was it all just a dream?" Michael Moore asks at the beginning of *Fahrenheit 9/11*. The chronic inflation in the public register, the anxiety of unreality, are constant companions in the political affairs of empire. Obama, who says he admires Reagan's ability to project transcendence, offers the same style of democratic glamour, abolishes the same differences between psychology and politics, celebrity and power. *The Audacity of Hope: Thoughts on Reclaiming the American Dream,* his second book, sidesteps the role of party standard-bearer in favor of dream-interpreter-in-chief. Here is the leader of and for our age, at once inhabiting the collective psyche and lending his personal vision to the spiritual quality of its longings.

REMEMBERING
RICHARD HOFSTADTER

Richard Hofstadter spent most his adult life in the "Upper West Side Kibbutz," an area of Morningside Heights bounded by Claremont Avenue, Riverside Drive and Columbia's Hamilton Hall. Of the eminences who inhabited this neighborhood in the 1950's—Daniel Bell, Peter Gay, Irving Kristol, Lionel Trilling—Hofstadter achieved the most impressive mix of critical and commercial success.

He published prodigiously: more than a dozen major books, collections and anthologies; a textbook that introduced thousands of college students to history; plus a handful of first-rate ruminations laid away in magazines and journals. *The American Political Tradition* (1948) sold 400,000 copies in its first two decades. *The Age of Reform* (1955) and *Anti-Intellectualism in American Life* (1963) each won the Pulitzer Prize. Even lesser volumes called out high praise. Gore Vidal described *The Paranoid Style in American Politics* (1965) as "a most engaging essay" and commended Hofstadter as one the "best contemporary critics" of "the collective madness of the electorate." In 1970, Hofstadter signed a contract with Knopf, his longtime publisher, for a three-volume history of American political culture. The trilogy was to take 18 years to complete, and was to earn the author $1.3 million in today's dollars, according to David Brown's *Richard Hofstadter: An Intellectual Biography*.

Hofstadter's reputation is strong among contemporary historians of the United States, and his books still sell briskly. Mr. Brown's biography should be welcomed accordingly. It's a quiet book for a quiet life: a childhood in Buffalo as the son of a Jewish father and a Lutheran mother; an early marriage to Felice Swados, a hot-blooded fellow student at the University of Buffalo; emigration to New York City in the middle of the Great Depression; a brief membership in the Communist Party; then, graduate school at Columbia, followed by a rise to prominence in the 1940's and 50's. No reversals, no scandals, no puzzling discrepancies, no purblind mistakes. From beginning to end, Hofstadter held the confidence of the center. In high school, he was both valedictorian and class president. In 1968, after Columbia University president Grayson Kirk discredited himself, it was Hofstadter who stepped forward to deliver the commencement address to the shattered campus. He's still the only member of the faculty so entrusted, according to Mr. Brown.

A moderate by temperament and an historian by training, Hofstadter was an intellectual by conviction. The animus of his thought set the life of the mind against "the populistic democracy." To the activist wing of the left, he resolved the conflict in favor of conservatism, for he insisted on the value of civility and on the need for institutions to uphold it. "In this age of rather overwhelming organizations and collectivities," he said at the 1968 commencement, "the university is singular in being a collectivity that serves as a citadel of intellectual individualism." To the activist wing of the right, he transformed dissent into pathology. "The Pseudo-Conservative Revolt," one of his early essays about McCarthyism, set out to explain "its dense and massive irrationality." But Hofstadter won his insights into the emotional roots of mass movements from a certain detachment from politics. "I can no longer describe myself as a radical," he said in a 1962 letter, "though I don't consider myself to be a conservative either. I suppose the truth is, although my interests are still very political, I none the less have no politics." One of his essays on the Goldwater insurgency, "The Contemporary Extreme Right Wing in the United States," carried an epigraph by Nietzsche on the "herd mentality."

Mr. Brown records Hofstadter's hypochondria and suggests that the premature deaths of his mother and first wife affirmed his natural melancholy. But the main incidents and sentiments of Hofstadter's life do not make for a very interesting portrait. The significance collects in the writings. Hofstadter was the postwar historian most respected by Trilling—and by Messrs. Bell, Gay and Kristol—because the quality of his convictions bespoke a traditional Jewish mistrust of passion in politics at a time when that mistrust seemed most necessary. The absence of dogmatism and jargon in his writings has attracted a variety of historians-as-cultural-critics. Eric Foner, a former student, has written admiringly about him. Arthur Schlesinger Jr. has observed that he was the first major historian to come out of New York City.

Hofstadter's anatomies of extremism can be read with much interest in our age of political hatred and culture war. Though it's rarely consulted in these days of furious party competition, the genre to which his work belongs has much to say about the decline of argument and the relationship between politics and emotion. Hofstadter's distinction was to marry the conceptual sophistication in such works as Harold Lasswell's *Psychopathology and Politics* and Theodor Adorno's *The Authoritarian Personality* with an unusually deft prose style. The portrait of John Calhoun etched in *The American Political Tradition*, for example, mixed the Marxist theory of false consciousness with a style attuned to irony and paradox. "Calhoun was a minority spokesman in a democracy, a particularist in an age of nationalism, a slaveholder in an age of advancing liberties, and an agrarian in a furiously capitalistic country. Quite understandably he developed a certain perversity of mind."

Hofstadter's method ("literary anthropology," he once called it) also commends him to us. He grew to maturity in the mid-1940's, alongside a generation of intellectuals searching for a style freed of the sectarian solemnity of the Depression decade. Dwight Macdonald titled a 1943 *Partisan Review* essay "A Rousseau for the NAM." Soon afterward, C. Wright Mills titled one of his essays "A Marx for the Managers." Hofstadter followed suit in *The American Political Tradition*, titling his chapter on Calhoun "The Marx of the Master Class." The book, a collection of biographical portraits, made Thomas Jefferson "The Aristocrat as Democrat" and Franklin Roosevelt "The Patrician as Opportunist," and so on. Academic historians read *The American Political Tradition* as a founding text in the consensus interpretation of politics, but it was the playful irreverence of the portraits, the mocking accent, which resounded in the public's ears. Hofstadter said of Calhoun: "There is no record that he ever read or tried to write poetry, although there is a traditional gibe to the effect that he once began a poem with 'Whereas,' and stopped."

David Brown calls Hofstadter "a modern-day Mencken," but like much else in this biography, he leaves the comparison to sit on the page with nothing much to do. Did Hofstadter and Mencken have anything in common? Mencken was an entertainer and a philistine who attacked the possibility of moral passion. Hofstadter was morally engaged in his times in positive as well as negative ways. Mencken drew all the wrong conclusions from his exposure to Herbert Spencer ("social Darwinism in shirtsleeves" was his philosophy, according to Terry Teachout). Hofstadter's first book, *Social Darwinism in American Thought*, praised the pragmatists for rescuing the theory of evolution from petit bourgeois bachelors like Mencken, who were always smacking people across the face with "survival of the fittest" slogans.

Still, there *is* a curious similarity in their cultural criticism. Probably no two writers did more damage to the reputation of prairie radicalism. *The American Political Tradition* attacked the populist leader William Jennings Bryan in the same urbane manner, and for many of the same reasons, as Mencken's famous obituary in the *American Mercury*. Of Bryan's 1896 campaign for the Presidency on a free-silver platform, Hofstadter quipped: "It was the only time in the history of the Republic when a candidate ran for presidency on the strength of a monomania." *The Age of Reform* returned to the subject with a vengeance. The book argued that, rather than being crushed by "the interests," the farmers had lacked the moral and imaginative resources by which to respond intelligently to the transformations wrought by industrialism. Hofstadter assailed the "pathetic postwar career of Bryan," bemoaned the "shabbiness of the evangelical mind," and dismissed rational grounds for the populist complaint. Mencken lampooned the genteel tradition for its unreality. Hofstadter set out to destroy the sentimental treatment of agrarian radicalism in the writings of Charles Beard and Frederick Jackson Turner.

The Columbia historian Alan Brinkley has called *The Age of Reform* "the most influential book ever published on the history of twentieth-century America." This is true but not necessarily salutary. Hofstadter's mockery made it possible for generations of urban liberals to sneer at the "folklore of populism" without confronting its criticisms of industrial capitalism, much as Mencken made it easy for generations of conservatives to mistake smartness for intelligence. Mr. Brown, interestingly, says Hofstadter later softened his attack on the farmers when he was confronted with evidence that anti-Semitism was as strong in the eastern cities as it had been in the Midwest. (If Hofstadter had learned of Mencken's own anti-Semitism, perhaps he would have made more such concessions.) In any case, the social thought of Christopher Lasch, a Hofstadter student, and the writings of Wendell Berry show that today's populism has developed considerably beyond its early racialism. One measure of *The Age of Reform's* influence lies in the large literature refuting it.

Hofstadter distributed his satire liberally, but not liberally enough to check the patronizing tone that crept into his style over time. The Beats, he wrote in 1962, "have produced very little good writing. Their most distinctive contribution to our culture may in the end be their amusing argot. The movement seems unable to rise above its adolescent inspiration." As the center dispersed in the strenuous 1960's, the absurdities of American politics sprouted new styles of satire and longing. Hofstadter kept his hair short and his bowtie tight. He suffered bouts of "intellectual confusion" (in Mr. Brown's words), much as Mencken grew disoriented when the fat targets of the 1920's made way for the realities of the 1930's.

Soon after he delivered the commencement address at Columbia, Hofstadter abandoned his home in the "Upper West Side Kibbutz" for a quieter spot on the East Side. In the summer of 1970, his three-volume work incomplete, he confided his disappointment in an interview with *Newsweek*. "I can't see much that is positive coming out of this period. If I get around to writing a general history of the recent past, I'm going to call the chapter on the 60's 'The Age of Rubbish.'" A few months later he died of leukemia. He was fifty-four.

PERSONAL PRAGMATISM

Biography's contribution to intellectual history depends on its ability to express relationships among formal ideas, personal qualities, and historical circumstances. Louis Menand's *The Metaphysical Club*—a collective biography that traces the origins of American pragmatism to the four decades after the Civil War—merits close inspection as a contribution to such a history.

In its pursuit of "changing assumptions," the book explores a stunning array of late nineteenth and early twentieth-century topics: Darwinism, American Transcendentalism, German Idealism, Statistics, Astronomy, abolitionism, assimilationism, nativism, labor unions, research universities, to name a few. Yet the narrative core of the book centers on the lives and ideas of four men: jurist Oliver Wendell Holmes, Jr., and philosophers Charles Peirce, William James, and John Dewey. These four shared and promoted a new attitude to human inquiry, captured, Menand says, in "an idea about ideas:" "they all believed that ideas are not 'out there' waiting to be discovered, but are tools—like forks and knives and microchips—that people devise to cope with the world in which they find themselves." Knowledge, according to this way of thinking, is socially produced by groups, not by individuals, and the survival of ideas in a culture depends not on their correspondence with the world, but their adaptability to prevailing circumstances.

How and why did Holmes, Peirce, James, and Dewey come to these conclusions? Menand's answer takes the form of a series of highly nuanced intellectual portraits, which give each of the four an idiosyncratic (but partly convergent) march of development that features their personalities alongside their ideas. The book contains a multitude of anecdotes—always interesting, sometimes fascinating—involving family background, social rank, political viewpoint, institutional position, professional jealousies, personal taste, private habit, and so on. For Menand, inclusiveness is a matter of intellectual method, not personal prurience. By presenting ideas as deeply embedded in circumstance—"soaked through by the personal and social situations in which we find them"—and not in splendid intellectual isolation, Menand has attempted to write a history of pragmatism on its own terms.

The pragmatists, he contends, "believed that ideas do not develop according to some inner logic of their own, but are entirely dependent, like germs, on their human carriers and the environment." Menand's interpretation of this claim puts special emphasis on "human carriers." His "story of ideas in America" is a record of distinctive personalities and biographical experiences. This dramatization of human culture helps explain *The Metaphysical Club*'s popular appeal: its biographical portraits make for terrific reading, and its success as popular history is assured. Most of the discussions surrounding the revival of pragmatism in modern American thought have remained within the universities. That Menand's book has already brought this complicated philosophical movement into the broader culture is no small achievement.

As a work of intellectual history, however, *The Metaphysical Club* leaves much to be desired. Because Menand roots pragmatism's development in the idiosyncratic personalities of its progenitors, he has trouble explaining how and why these different thinkers converged on a set of tightly related ideas. He strains to emphasize two biographical experiences that all four men are said to have shared—the American Civil War and the brief-lived metaphysical club of the title—but neither explanation is compelling. Moreover, by so thoroughly locating pragmatism in specific personalities and biographies, Menand diminishes his ability to explain it as a set of ideas with broad contemporary significance.

■■■

Dramatic episodes of the Civil War introduce *The Metaphysical Club,* and lay the groundwork for Menand's interpretation of pragmatism as a philosophical reaction to the conflict's absolutist temper. "Holmes, James, Peirce, and Dewey wished to bring ideas and principles and beliefs down to a human level because they wished to avoid the violence they saw hidden in abstractions," Menand insists. "This was one of the lessons the Civil War had taught them." Thus, Oliver Wendell Holmes, Jr., a Union soldier, came to regard the war as the "central experience" of his life and the fulcrum of his philosophical obligations to uncertainty. A participant in some exceptionally bloody battles, the thrice-wounded Holmes thereafter carried deep physical and emotional scars. Eventually, as Menand puts it, the war "changed his view of the nature of views," and "made him lose his belief in beliefs."

But Menand's subsequent efforts to keep alive the moral tension of the war and its intellectual impact frequently seem forced. When the youthful William James decided to accompany Harvard zoologist Louis Agassiz on an expedition to Brazil, he was, according to Menand, actually choosing to serve in the war, "in a sense." Joining with Agassiz, who was constructing a polygenic hierarchy of the races, meant, furthermore, that James had chosen "the wrong side." Menand likewise strains for links between John Dewey's ideas and the Civil War, finding little more than the fact that his father, Archibald Dewey, enlisted on the side of the North, served for the duration, and remained a committed Republican throughout his life.

The blood of the war may well have washed away Holmes's early faith in the certainty of abolitionism, and any other certainty: "Time," Holmes said in dissent in *Abrams v. U.S.,* "has upset many fighting faiths." But the "great lesson he thought the war had taught him," did not directly apply to the others, including his friend William James. Indeed, Menand's evidence on the role of the Civil War is sometimes so scanty that he compels tattered analogies into service. On the trip to Brazil, James endured "a sort of wound:" smallpox. As for Dewey, Menand links his development as a pragmatic intellectual to conversations with reformer Jane Addams about the Pullman strike, another of the seemingly intractable political and moral conflicts faced by late-nineteenth century thinkers. That Dewey would be so interested in public affairs in the first place, Menand suggests, owes to a lesson imparted by the Civil War. Only this lesson seems opposite Holmes's. Immediately after explaining Archibald Dewey's soldierly enthusiasms, Menand indicates that John Dewey was raised "in a family with a culture of social commitment." His father was a "die-hard Republican all his life." On Menand's evidence, Archibald Dewey not only appears to embrace precisely the kind of principled certainties that Holmes most distrusted, but also appears to have transmitted these values to his son.

Such complications make Menand's interpretative focus on the war unconvincing. The book's opening pages make Northern abolitionism stand generally for the toxicity of grand ideas. By the book's end, abolitionism stands as a trope. The war imbues the story with a sense of drama, though it seems less able to explain the emergence of pragmatism as a sustained, collective phenomenon.

If a shared reaction to the Civil War does not account for pragmatism's common appeal to thinkers with such distinct personalities and perspectives, neither does shared membership in a short-lived Metaphysical Club in Cambridge. The reader who flips through two hundred pages to find the contribution made by the club will find that for two of the book's principal figures it had only slight intellectual significance. Holmes was "probably not a frequent participant in the Metaphysical Club discussions," and "James did not need the Metaphysical Club to reach his conclusion about the nature of beliefs." The presence of Charles Peirce and fellow-philosopher Chauncey Wright (whose alcoholism is presented as the decisive factor in his philosophical failings) furnishes the most compelling reasons for Menand to present the 'founding' of the club as a landmark in the long history of pragmatism. Yet even Peirce and Wright had "fought out nearly a thousand close disputations, regular set-tos concerning the philosophy of [John Stuart] Mill...before the Metaphysical Club had been started." Perhaps, Menand finally says, the club never existed in the first place.

Menand repeatedly strains historical and philosophical interpretation in the service of personalized animation. While he provides an ample account of Charles Peirce's struggle with the indeterminacy of meaning and the fallibility of convictions, his faith in the personal context leads him to push Peirce's published writings on the topic aside, in search of a biographical moment of cohesion. "What does it mean," Menand asks, "to say that a statement is 'true' in a world always susceptible to 'a certain swerving'?" Then he offers an entirely speculative answer: "Peirce got a hint of how this question might be answered from another member of the Metaphysical Club, Nicholas St. John Green." Carried along by Green's critique of the legal concept of "proximate cause"—so the story runs—Peirce was inspired to write a paper about the "practical bearings" of human inquiry that he read during the final meeting of the club. Or did he? Menand cannot say for sure, yet he indicates that the reading of that paper came to occupy the center of pragmatic thinking, its contents—later elaborated in Peirce's "How To Make Our Ideas Clear"—quickly spreading to the others through channels direct and indirect. That no record exists to document the club's activities—other than Peirce's own fragmented recollection—means that Peirce may have read virtually anything.

More important than the specific conclusions that Menand draws from the war or from the presumed existence of The Metaphysical Club, the burden of the book's biographical arguments—which locate causal relationships from within the immediate spheres of these thinkers's lives—makes personal epiphany a motor of intellectual development. Such personal revelation is fine as far as it goes, but often it fails to move ideas far enough away from the individual thinker to allow them free play.

The most satisfying moments in *The Metaphysical Club* occur when the emotional arc of one of the characters meets the

articulation of an idea. When Holmes is discovered metamorphos-
ing his war-time experiences into a philosophy of jurisprudence,
for instance. Or when Charles Peirce and his famous father, the
Harvard mathematician Benjamin Peirce, partner as expert witnesses
in a celebrated trial, *Robinson v. Mandell.* The Peirces, according
to Menand, used the occasion of their 1867 testimony to test and
promote the "law of errors," the same analytic tool that would become central to Charles's social theory of knowledge.

Even during such moments, however, one is pulled back and
forth between edification and enlightenment. Menand's efforts to
contextualize pragmatism in a web of personal, social, and intellectual sensibilities compete with the reader's efforts to understand
pragmatism as a body of ideas that evolves, enlightens, and succeeds
(or fails) on its own terms. Menand often seems too impressed by
the intimate cocktail party of nineteenth-century intellectual life,
with all its coincidences and connections, and insufficiently attentive to argument. A typical passage begins: "In 1888, on a train to
Cleveland to attend a scientific meeting, [Franz] Boas got into a
conversation with the man in the seat next to him, who, at the end
of the trip, offered him a job. The friendly passenger was G. Stanley
Hall, recruiting for the newly opened Clark University. Boas taught
at Clark for four years," and so on. Serendipity adds much to the
book's aesthetic feel, little to its explanatory power.

No doubt, by recasting some of the action in pragmatism's
development from its abstract philosophical inheritance to odd
personalities, wars, and lawsuits, Menand offers readers a story
that is sometimes both thrilling and illuminating. Equally certain,
though, this "story of ideas" is often overwhelmed by a thicket of
personality and circumstance. Consider, for example, Menand's
portrayal of the animosity between critic Randolph Bourne and
his former teacher, John Dewey. Menand observes that Dewey
became angry over Bourne's review of a book to which Dewey
had contributed an introduction, then records Dewey's support
for war in 1917 (the occasion for their feud). He says in summary
of both topics: "[Dewey's] momentary advocacy of violent means

during the First World War is a peculiar episode in his career, but his reaction to the Alexander review is even more peculiar." His displeasure at Bourne may seem "peculiar," given Dewey's mild-mannered disposition and his failure to realize that Alexander's book might affront Bourne for personal reasons. But do Dewey's support for the war and his personal insensitivity issue from the same kind of "peculiar?" Are these two instances of Dewey's intellectual character really so commensurable?

Engaging with his pragmatism in its own right is vital to judging its merits, not least because Dewey's support for World War I can hardly be understood as "momentary." Menand could have represented the relationship between Dewey's pragmatist philosophical commitments and his wartime politics in any number of ways. A contradiction? A logical entailment? An elective affinity? Almost anything would improve "peculiar," a characterization that permits no real response.

Not only do broad, historical explanations become more difficult to sustain as Menand descends to the idiosyncratic details of private life, but his focus on those details does not aid evaluation of pragmatism as a philosophical outlook. To be sure, such blurring of contexts constitutes a purposeful aspect of Menand's contribution to intellectual biography, his "point about the nature of intellectual culture." But certainly there are other ways to historicize pragmatism, equally attentive to its contextual scruples, that seem more conducive to the task of intellectual assessment.

▐▐▐

In 1942, C. Wright Mills, then a 26-year-old sociologist fresh from the University of Wisconsin, completed an intellectual history of pragmatism from a perspective that also emphasized the social character of knowledge. Mills considered the pragmatists to be his intellectual "godfathers." The major gestures and problems of his post-war social criticism, expressed in popular books such as *White Collar* (1951) and *The Power Elite* (1956), issued from a commitment to their anti-metaphysical premises. Yet it is Mills's earliest work, "A Sociological Account of Pragmatism," that best

illuminates by contrast what is lost in Menand's highly personalized approach to the subject.

"A Sociological Account of Pragmatism" argued that to understand the work of Peirce, Dewey, and James one must certainly
understand their biographies—the "human carriers and the environment." More specifically though, one must know how their
biographies intersected with the decisive, large-scale changes in
American social structure that shaped and sustained their ideas.
Mills argued that Dewey's experimentalist pragmatism developed
out of his institutional contacts with skilled tradesmen, scientists,
and newly professionalized teachers—each of whom inhabited a
dynamic occupational context that required the flexible use of intelligence, rational thinking, and manipulation of symbolic material.
His account ascribed Dewey's pragmatism neither to the intellectual
sensibilities of the man nor to the "inner logic" of his philosophical
inheritance. Nonetheless it successfully demonstrated the social
and moral relevance of the pragmatist experiment. By offering his
reading public access to different, developing spheres of social and
professional life, Mills argued, Dewey "helped build and worked
within the increased spread of ascent chances for the sons of farmers
and businessmen into professional careers." From above, he encountered the "new educational managers and the gilded philanthropists
who were the financial midwives" for the research universities of the
late nineteenth century—that is, for the new universities where he
taught. Beside him emerged a new class of students and academi-
cians, people moving upward in a more fluid economy and society.
Epochal transformations in American occupational structure
"formed the scaffolding for many newly founded institutions" that
formed, in turn, the scaffolding for Dewey's pragmatism. Such were
its "direct determinants," according to Mills.

Menand writes compellingly of the universities of Vermont,
Michigan, and Chicago, of Harvard, Johns Hopkins, Columbia
and of other institutional bulwarks of the new professional social
structure. But even here, Menand reverses Mills's priorities. The
sociologist insisted that "the mechanics and structures which

set the institutional base of an intellectual milieu 'go on behind the backs' of the individuals participating in them." The literary critic represents ideas through the transits of the intentional, the breezily personal.

▐▐▐

The most important consequences of contrasting "A Sociological Account of Pragmatism" and *The Metaphysical Club*—otherwise complementary projects—surpass the dissimilarities between the academic disciplines of sociology and English. Mills and Menand each have a popular appeal that transcends their respective disciplinary boundaries.

Within a decade after Mills completed his examination of the subject, he contended that American pragmatism could no more become a renewed "nerve of progressive thinking" than Victorian Marxism. Mills had argued that Dewey's experimental theory of action was tested upon those "free professionals" who were "predominately outside the rationalized structures in which the action of individuals faces decisions, and almost by definition, decisions involving new factors that have come into the actor's horizon and path." A decline in the substantive rationality available to Dewey's white-collar professional publics meant a decline in opportunities for his theory of action. (Mills subsequently traced this decline in *White Collar.*) Mills's influential search for a radical social philosophy, however, held fast to the first premise that guided his early work: since structures and institutions exercised determinate power across American civilization, it was structures and institutions that deserved critical examination. In this conviction Mills joined an entire postwar generation concerned to know how the "institutional bases of intellectual life" affected its basic assumptions and problems.

The Metaphysical Club reflects the distance traveled by our public intellectuals from these assumptions. By so emphasizing personal qualities, Menand asks less of his subjects as thinkers, and so less of his readers as critics. Unlike Mills, he finds himself at book's end with no criteria clear enough to mount a firm evaluation. Though he notes, in his epilogue, the powerful reemergence of pragmatism at the end of the Cold War, and, thus, suggests such evaluation is of more than historical interest, he fails to help contemporary readers assess pragmatism's reduction of truth to efficacy—of the correctness of an outlook to its usefulness in our lives. "Whether this nineteenth-century way of thinking really does have twenty-first-century uses is not yet clear," he concludes after four hundred and forty pages of discussion. The absence of an incisive critical sensibility owes in part to Menand's personalization of the philosophical. Personal dispositions—William James' indecisiveness, Dewey's amiabil-ity—are walled off from criticism because, unlike institutions and occupations, they are not collectively and publicly and historically transmitted; criteria for evaluating them do not readily materialize. When ideas are so closely fastened to what Menand calls "unre-producible personalities," the reader gains few resources for critical judgment. Menand does offer a consideration of pragmatism's merits and deficiencies. But his evaluation of Holmes, James, Dewey, and Peirce as thinkers, compressed into a few summary sections, tends to take the form of declarative statements that carry synoptic modi-fiers such as "at bottom," "boils down," and "fundamentally." The problem is not that his evaluations are necessarily wrong; it is that they are pressed to the margins.

Menand's book flatters a present sensibility that offers little place for big ideas or independent moral judgment, but reserves many seats for dramatic personalities. The biography of intellectu-als, thus conceived, is concerned with imputation and exposition at the expense of criticism and argument. As Mills showed, a certain narrowing of conceptual space between biographical circumstances and formalized ideas can perform the act of unmasking, illumi-nating thinker and thought in lights that make both available to criticism. Too much light and too little heat, however, can invite historical spectatorship.

INFORMATION JUNKIES

I still remember the feeling of anticipation when I spread open *The New York Times* for the first time. I was 26 years old. I had been raised in rural Pennsylvania in a family of tradition-minded conservatives with little good to say about cities or their newspapers. Not until after I graduated from college in rural Virginia did I read *The Washington Post,* and it took a few more years to gin up the confidence to confront the *Times.*

More than any one story, the seriousness of mood struck me force-fully. "They'll never get away with it now!" I remember thinking to myself while reading the exposés of malfeasance and corruption. Since then I discovered the necessity of untruth in party-organized politics and the impossibility of finding rational grounds for value judgments. I learned to distrust the assumption that truth checks lies.

If the newspaper was not what it appeared to a rural naïf in the mid-1990s, already it was giving way to another kind of anticipation. Even before I left college I heard bold predictions that the Internet would make newspapers obsolete. Today those predictions form a consensus that, if realized, promises to make my generation witness to a profound transformation. Yet the most striking feature of this transformation is not a radical break between old and new media; it is the underlying continuity.

■■■

Only a sudden interruption of daily newspaper reading could expose its ritualistic quality. Thus, the significance of the New York news-paper strike of June 30, 1945, during which eight major dailies were not delivered for 17 days. In a famous essay on reader's reactions to the strike, "What 'Missing the Newspaper' Means," behavioral scientist Bernard Berelson reported a diffuse panic in the public. Almost everyone he and his team interviewed claimed to miss the "serious information" contained in the newspaper, yet few of the respondents could recall any specific stories or events they had been following prior to the strike. Berelson concluded that what they really missed was "the ritualistic and near-compulsive character of newspaper reading." The longer the strike went on, the more people missed that feeling. This acute psychological dependency, so often noticed by critics of mass media, was intrinsic to the enterprise from the beginning.

⬛⬛⬛

The newspaper emerged with the anomie of modern society. To the displaced and disorganized, it offered an illusion of solidarity, a chance to participate vicariously in social knowledge by sharing gossip. By the middle of the 20th century, newspapers presented themselves both as a guides to the management of self (offering weather and financial forecasts, advertisements for commodities, records of births, deaths, marriages, and events) and as vehicles of escape from the banality of self-management (sports, comics, scandals, crises, human-interest stories). In truth, the newspaper offered another routine for a society of estranged individuals afraid to be alone with their thoughts and feelings.

The news never stopped. Every issue introduced a new crisis or scandal into the same eternal present of repetitive triviality. The critic Dwight Macdonald noted the self-aggrandizing quality of the information cult, whose real subject was attention. "For those who, as readers or as writers, would get a little under the surface, the real problem of our day is how to escape being 'well informed,' how to resist the temptation to acquire too much information (never more seductive than when it appears in the chaste garb of duty), and how in general to elude the voracious demands on one's attention enough to think a little."

The migration of the public from print to the Internet carries the same ritual psychology of slavish dependence. On April 17,

2007, millions of BlackBerrys in North America suddenly stopped working. Cut off from their wireless email system for a few hours, users reported feeling phantom vibrations and compared the effect to a forced drug withdrawal. Berelson would have understood, just as Macdonald would have understood how the high-blown rhetoric of information and citizenship that accompanies the Internet hides the fact that it often discourages the very qualities of mind and character needed to think clearly and independently.

The Internet is completing the newspaper's project of seizing mass attention. In the absence of real solidarity, it multiplies the technological functions of the psyche. Often the results are felt as a minor irony: While the machine makes communicating more efficient, it dramatically increases the volume of communication.

The feeling of technical power, moreover, generates no equivalent political or moral resources. Terrorists create manuals that instruct fanatics how to use the Internet for recruitment, strategy, and propaganda. In China and elsewhere, technology is easily adapted to the needs of authoritarian regimes—and the corporations that provide it are eager to comply. Does the Internet bring friends together? It also brings together spammers, spies, and misanthropes who find and exploit new tools of seduction and surveillance. The mob mentality, always a danger in democracies, is no longer organized around the newspaper; now it finds itself online.

Not only public and private, but the human distinctions of home and away, past and present, here and there, are abolished in the bleary cries of More and Now. Once civilized man regarded the machine as an extension to his power. Then, man worried that he had become a slave to the machinery of civilization that he had created. Now, man becomes the machine's facsimile: disciplined, regular, undivided. Gone and going is the image of the person as an organic being, emerging, growing, decaying, returning. In the virtual world, as in the world of the print newspaper, the difference between communing and communicating goes unrecognized. Convenience is an unmixed good; solitude the stigmata of eccentrics and loners.

As all spheres of practical life go online, with or without the consent of the connected, as possibilities turn into necessities, vicarious participation in society grows more burdensome as it grows more abstract. The romantic idea of the Internet as the summation of individual wills united in voluntary association has been replaced by a paradox characteristic of the utopian ego. Freedom of choice does not acknowledge the most important choice of all: the freedom to sign off.

III

HISTORY AS BIOGRAPHY

THE BIG DISCOURSE

L oneliness burdens most college freshmen, though precious few find lasting relief from it in the realm of ideas. So it happened for one freshman in 1935, when he left behind the isolation he had experienced at Texas A&M for the University of Texas and "the big discourse," his term for the Enlightenment humanism that extended him both refuge and inspiration. Once a diffident student, he quickly gave to this tradition the allegiance of an apostle. At age 20, he wrote his father: "I work and live very rapidly these days. Mine is a pen from whose point much ink will flow and some day into the brains of the populace. But let that be."

Much ink did flow from the pen of C. Wright Mills. As a professor of sociology at Columbia University, Mills wrote pro- digiously throughout the forties and fifties, publishing in major newspapers and journals of opinion and in *little magazines* in equal measure. Two of his books, *White Collar* (1951) and *The Power Elite* (1956), sold widely outside the academy, exerting a profound influence on the early New Left. A heart attack in March 1962 cut short his life at 45 years, but ten books and nearly 200 articles, essays and reviews had won him an international reputation. His books are now translated into twenty-three languages.

Mills departed Austin in 1939 for doctoral work at the Uni- versity of Wisconsin. Two years later, he completed a dissertation that fused the pragmatist philosophy he had learned at Texas with his new métier, sociology. "A Sociological Account of Pragmatism" disappointed him. Yet that dissertation, and particularly three innovative articles on the sociology of knowledge that preceded it, impressed influential members of the profession. In December 1940 Robert Merton, himself a theorist only six years Mills' senior, privately named him one of the three most promising sociologists in the nation.

A young prince in a rising discipline, Mills accepted an associate professorship of sociology at the University of Maryland, but he turned much of his attention to the lonely task of left-wing political agitation. In these years, anxieties over a permanent war economy traveled among New York's socialist community, to which Mills began to appeal for contacts, and his political writings expressed fear that monopoly capitalism was generating a proto-fascist domestic apparatus underwritten by cultural insensibility and mass discipline.

Sensitive to the fast-changing character of liberal social structure, Mills held out against the irony of reform. Unlike so many of his elders, he did not know firsthand the capacity of entrenched power to co-opt and redirect dissent; nor had he suffered the lost promises of international Communism. "I did not personally experience the thirties. At that time, I just didn't get its mood," he explained in one of the 150 letters published in *C. Wright Mills: Letters and Autobiographical Writings*, a beautifully edited volume by Kathryn Mills with Pamela Mills (his daughters). "Only with the onset of World War II did I become radically aware of public affairs."

Released from military duty because of hypertension, Mills viewed the war as "a goddamned bloodbath to no end save misery and mutual death to all civilized values." He harbored no sympathy for the scars of erstwhile agitators. In an essay published in 1942 in the *New Leader*, he observed that their chastened radicalism belonged to a more thoroughgoing "crisis in American pragmatism," in which private religious introspection, not political action, now served as the preferred sphere for the full development of the human personality. This kind of retreat into religion, Mills complained, neglected a "social theory of the self" (which he had explored in his early writings on the sociology of knowledge). It left individuals intellectually powerless to influence the massive secular forces that now overwhelmed them. The move away from politics, Mills wrote, "offers a personal and accommodative celebration of the modern fact of self-estrangement." (Similarly, he would later christen the "cult of alienation" that enveloped postwar literature as "a fashionable way of being overwhelmed.") Already by 1942, he regarded commitment to humanist politics and ideas as a spiritual enterprise that demanded steadiness of public purpose in the face of illiberal forces. This disposition, part evangelical, part stoic, would thereafter guide his criticism of US institutions.

Mills published widely during the mid- and late-forties, furthering his reputation for precocity even while shifting his research interests from the sociology of knowledge to stratification, labor, and social psychology. In 1945, an invitation arrived from Paul Lazarsfeld to join the Bureau of Applied Social Research at Columbia University, and he left College Park for New York.

The New Men of Power appeared three years later, the first fruit of Mills' work for the bureau. Surveying the origins, attitudes and party affiliations of 500 labor leaders, the book aspired to an objective, collective portrait that would also become politically relevant. "The most democratic societies of their size in the world," labor unions, he concluded, nonetheless possessed the tendencies of the political economy that had shaped them: the elaboration of hierarchy and bureaucracy, the exclusive reliance on the major parties, the nervous impulse to conserve recent gains, the demotion of labor intellectuals to the role of gadfly or technician. Could labor leaders, whom Mills called a new "strategic elite" in the contest for power, resist "the main drift"?

Somewhat like the labor leaders he studied, Mills was managing a host of positions and influences in his thought. *The New Men of Power* contained traces of Wisconsin progressivism, Trotskyist socialism, a concept of "publics" imported from John Dewey, new techniques of social science research, even the rebellious spirit of the Wobblies. This pluralism made possible a salutary absence of dogmatism, and the book gathered reviews appreciative of its political energy and broad vision. He finished, though, with an ambivalent note on the prospects for an accord between labor leaders and labor intellectuals, which he thought vital for any recrudescence of independent politics: "Never has so much depended upon men who are so ill-prepared and so little inclined to assume the responsibility."

White Collar marked a rapidly maturing social theory. It also commenced Mills' rise to a peculiar place in American intellectual life. Although professional sociologists greeted the book with indifference or distrust, others hailed it as a provocative examination of the psychology of class. It became a bestseller, evidence that independent radicalism could find a place even during the dark nights of McCarthyism.

Mills, in turn, looked with growing confidence outside his profession for authority as a critic. Over the course of the decade, Cold War dissidents and uneasy students repaid his efforts in direct proportion to his escalating boldness. "I can no longer write seriously without feeling contempt for the indifferent professors and smug editors of the overdeveloped societies in the West who so fearlessly fight the cold war, and for the cultural bureaucrats and hacks, the intellectual thugs of the official line," he wrote in *The Causes of World War Three* (1958), an antiwar pamphlet that sold 100,000 copies. In *Listen Yankee* (1960), a pro-Castro polemic that sold more than 400,000 copies, Mills called the United States a "reactionary menace" and proclaimed his independence from the growing student movement that drew inspiration from his example. "I cannot give unconditional loyalties to any institution, man, state, movement, or nation. My loyalties are conditional upon my own convictions and my own values."

As the New Left gathered momentum, Mills seemed the man for the moment. Agitating for "our own separate peace," with Communist intellectuals, he made official visits to Cuba and the USSR, traded counsel with Sartre in France, talked up E.P. Thompson to the Cubans and Carlos Fuentes to US publishers. One year before his fatal heart attack, he wrote to his parents about the obligations he supposed his writings had brought him. "I know now that I have not the slightest fear of death; I know also that I have a big responsibility to thousands of people all over the world to tell the truth as I see it and to tell it exactly and with drama and quit this horsing around with sociological bullshit." A self-proclaimed "permanent stranger" in a nation he could not leave, Mills died a triply distinctive figure of US culture: a radical intellectual celebrity.

To many of his colleagues, he appeared an abrasive and even irresponsible sociologist, his contentious manner unworthy of the detached, scientific ideals to which their discipline aspired. The body of literature that now surrounds Mills is generally distinguished only by its tendency to respond to this outsized reputation and audacious personality, rather than to the ideas they illustrated.

Such is the guiding spirit of *Collaboration, Reputation, and Ethics in American Academic Life* by sociologists Guy Oakes and Arthur Vidich. Oakes and Vidich recount the bitter disputes between Mills and the refugee sociologist Hans Gerth, his friend and collaborator on two books, *Character and Social Structure* (1953), a textbook, and *From Max Weber* (1946), an influential collection of Weber translations. Mills and Gerth quarreled incessantly over credit and control of these works. Theirs was a complicated relationship that Oakes and Vidich reduced to a cynical, one-dimensional interpretation aimed at little more than proving Mills a charlatan and misanthrope. Though *Collaboration, Reputation, and Ethics in American Academic Life* claims to make a minor advance in "the history of academic ethics," it fails to discuss prevailing standards of scholarly publishing in a fast-changing academy, standards against which we might measure the issues involved. Instead, Oakes and Vidich draw inferences from a batch of letters, some of them missing pages, and from an incomplete account of Mills' swift rise to prominence. Placing him in the worst possible light at every turn, they refuse to offer readers the opportunity to reach conclusions contrary to their own.

The competing portraits of Mills as leftist hero and Mills as academic villain caricature a stubbornly complex man. They fix his character within the very roles that he tried to elude or combine, imposing evaluative criteria that disregard his own terms of self-understanding. Insofar as they attribute his ideas to his eccentric personality they deradicalize the work. What remains to be explored, among those who would take his books with their intended seriousness, are the reasons for his popularity.

Throughout the fifties, Mills, borrowing freely from Dewey, Lippmann and Mead no less than from Veblen, Marx and Weber, returned to a theme that connected him to the decade's subterranean rumblings: the abstracted character of postwar life. Mills thought the United States, an "overdeveloped" supersociety, fattened on a feast of decayed symbols, which offered only outdated fragments of "the whole of live experience." Public life, therefore, yielded not morally relevant ideas but tremulous moods and slogans. It produced not craftsmen but "cheerful robots," not the means to use civil liberties but a rhetoric in their abstracted defense, not leaders of reason but paeans to the reasonableness of leadership. Massive, centralized institutions had arisen ("big, ugly forces"), by "drift" and by "thrust" alike. Yet corresponding pictures of reality failed to amplify what terrible challenges these institutions posed to "genuinely lively things."

Mills argued that white-collar workers and other Americans, bereft of reliable firsthand portraits of everyday reality, suffered confusion and powerlessness, trapped by the detritus of outworn images fixed in the social worlds of the eighteenth and nineteenth centuries. In national politics, a dominant liberalism did not suffocate alternatives, as some Marxists believed. Rather, a "liberal rhetoric" diverted attention from a more important thought: There existed no coherent ideologies of any sort to connect the universalist ideals transmitted by liberalism and Marxism to the colossal social structures that now overwhelmed them. Reason and freedom did not inevitably increase, as the progressive teleologies assumed. But no satisfactory projects for the modern realization of these ideals had evolved accordingly. Now, they suffered eclipse before the impersonal forces of bureaucratization, centralization and rationalization so characteristic of a mass society. "The big discourse" stood homeless.

Alive to this gap separating experience and consciousness, Mills suggested, opportunistic elites appropriated and managed "second-hand worlds" in the service of a pecuniary standard of value. The money standard, the only measure of value permitted to flourish, in turn made possible the commodity culture that spun ever faster around the axis of the US class structure. "Images of American types have not been built carefully by piecing together live experience," he remarked in *White Collar*. "Experience is trapped by false images, even as reality itself sometimes seems to imitate the soap opera and the publicity release." The "tang and feel" of American life meant "shrill trivialization" of culture by the mass media and hypnotic manipulation of psychic existence by moneyed elites. Workers had become possessed by the logic of "personality markets." Mills said citizens were "strangers to politics...not radical, not liberal, not conservative, not reaction-ary; they are inactionary; they are out of it." Even leisure, where people might expect to revivify their creative instincts, betrayed its promise. The absence of pictures of reality, autonomous from the commodity nexus, allowed only formal options emptied of real substance. "The most important characteristic of all these [leisure] activities is that they astonish, excite, and distract but they do not enlarge reason or feeling, or allow spontaneous dispositions to unfold creatively."

Much the same attack on formalism propelled *The Power Elite*, Mills' "good loud blast at the bastards, one they can't ignore maybe." The selection and formation of leaders in government, business and the military, he argued, occurred within social worlds narrowly circumscribed by the values of money and militarism. The prep school, the corporate hierarchy, the "total way of life" of the military regimen: Each of these transits to power lacked clearly articulated, open rules of advancement, instead fostering social and psychological affinities "designed to form members that will tacitly accept and trust and respect one another." Thus imbued with class consciousness, this power elite pursued the major "command posts" of modern American society.

Merely to assert in the fifties that an American upper class existed meant to court controversy. Mills went much further. Long-term trends in US social structure, he maintained, had both enlarged and consolidated the "command posts" occupied by the elite. "Local society," its business and Congressional retinue, had suffered a fatal decline. Now, the higher officer corps, the administrative apparatus surrounding the presidency and a corporate hierarchy of the "very rich" exercised international power of unprecedented scope. Professional politicians had abdicated their responsibility to make this power responsive. Increasingly, a quasi-official "political directorate" of businessmen and military "warlords" appropriated the "executive centers of decision."

That an elite possessed such immense power at all should distress any democrat, Mills seemed to suggest. That it exercised such power on behalf of private, self-interested standards of value should cause outrage. Within the "second-hand worlds" that determined public consciousness, the requirements of America's permanent war economy foreclosed alternative views. Pluralism, the dominant but now outdated picture of US democracy, only muddled the origins of the "moral uneasiness of our time": the dimly perceived understanding that the power elite adhered to a "crackpot realism," "a paranoid reality all their own" that might produce the most terrible of results: a third world war.

The Sociological Imagination (1959) continued Mills' assault on bourgeois formalism, focusing attention on prevailing models of social science. "Until now I have not really fought these people in American sociology," he wrote the British socialist Ralph Miliband late in the decade. "I've ignored them and done my own work; but they've been fooling around behind the scenes and now I declare war: I am going to expose their essential bankruptcy." By "behind the scenes" Mills was alluding, one supposes, to his own department. For his book expressed and then sought to surmount the major fault lines in professional social science at Columbia and other leading departments.

"Grand Theory," said Mills, offering a witty "translation" of the jargon-laden prose of Harvard sociologist Talcott Parsons, was afflicted by a formalist withdrawal from actual problems of the world. The grand theorists trafficked in a self-referential realm of reflection dominated by minute distinctions and interminable elaborations of basic concepts. In ascending to their "useless heights" they presupposed a natural harmony of ideas—their "metaphysical anchor point"—and so regarded conflict as a deviant phenomenon to be explained, not assumed. Yet because Parsons "has fetishized his Concepts," the exercise of power in real-world situations could not very well make its way into his work in the first place, nor into that of other grand theorists. "The basic cause of grand theory is the initial choice of a level of thinking so general that its practitioners cannot logically get down to observation. They never, as grand theorists, get down from the higher generalities to problems in their historical and structural contexts. This absence of a firm sense of genuine problems, in turn, makes for the unreality so noticeable in their pages."

"Abstracted Empiricism," too, constituted a withdrawal from substantive problems. Possessed by method, the empirical studies of Paul Lazarsfeld yielded a great many details about attitudes and opinions of social life, though such studies "do not convince us of anything worth having convictions about." Their frame of reference, according to Mills, usually remained so narrow and precise as to deny the fruits of empirical data any larger connection to social structure. "There is, in truth, no principle or theory that guides the selection of what is to be the subject of these studies," he remarked. Abstracted empiricism, an approach that aspired to put sociology on a particular type of scientific basis, shrank from the task of moral and political judgment. The "formal and empty ingenuity at its center," not to mention the basic requirements of its operations—large, well-funded research institutes—had turned

sociologists into mere technicians, solicitous of only the most immediate questions of the day.

Throughout his career Mills offered figures such as Veblen,
Balzac, Agee and Huizinga as models of inquiry, because they "took
it big"—took in the "whole of experience" and thereby sought to
stand apart from their milieu. In *The Sociological Imagination*,
Mills lamented that modern social science was, in the first and
final instance, connected only to the upper reaches of American
society. From there came the funding for the research institute,
the bureaucratic organization and specialized character of the
university; from there, he said, came the very definitions of the
problems of study. Mass society had rendered equivocal reason
and freedom. Now, without an intellectually autonomous class of
thinkers who made plain the political and ethical features of this
condition, society promised only to continue its fearful trajectory
toward a postmodern epoch. Mills implored his colleagues to connect history to biography, the private troubles of ordinary folks to
publicly relevant issues.

He left too little opportunity in his social psychology for the
formation of private consciousness, and his portraits often seemed
overdrawn accordingly. Today, his white-collar man implies a
comparison not to George Babbitt but instead to Hannah Arendt's
Adolf Eichmann. *The Power Elite* concluded darkly, shadowed by
the specter of US totalitarianism. To the extent that these books
stimulated the impulse to act, such inspiration owed not to precept
but to example, to the fact of their existence.

So it was for Mills' criticism of his colleagues: his moral
psychology and political hope outran his sociology. Much of his
work situated the creative individual within a web of psychic manipulation and centripetal forces. When he denounced his fellow
intellectuals as "futilitarians," then, his complaints seemed mere
hectoring. Late in the fifties he began to write more positively about
"cultural workmen" as agents of change and "the cultural apparatus" as a site of progressive advance. He never developed these
sentiments, however, and left important questions unanswered. In

challenging the monopolization of secondhand worlds by class-conscious elites, why should intellectuals be trusted to contain their own instinct for power?

Might Mills' calls for the transcendence of distinctions between culture and politics trivialize public life? He did not live to answer such questions fully. What is clear is that an elitism stood behind his writings. "Who wants to be loved by masses, or by mass-like minds?" he asked his longtime friend William Miller in 1954. In the end, his belief in intellectuals as an agent of social change became a modern version of the "labor metaphysic" he rejected in Victorian Marxism, as historian Michael Denning has noted.

Yet the tenacious exhortation for intellectuals to seek "publics" over masses constituted a strength, too. It belongs to his venture to make "reason democratically relevant," as he put the matter in *The Sociological Imagination*. Appreciating Mills' achievement in this respect does not require a sacrifice of the intellect, as his most parsimonious critics insist. Nobody did more to revive popular discussions of class and democracy in the postwar years. Nor did anyone make a more compelling bid to connect politics and ideas and "the whole of live experience" at a time when none of these seemed very compelling.

Mills refused to abandon universalist values even when his investigations disclosed ample reasons for doubting their continued relevance. If this grim perseverance could lead to a kind of elitism, it could also imbue his books with rhetorical force. Much of the power of his books and essays owes to the way in which he mined various traditions and impulses—liberal progress, Weberian irony, Texas populism, modern views of the sociology of knowledge—in the service of a near-missionary rhetoric of humanist redemption.

In a sense, a conservative radicalism anchored his life. He reported himself a member of the "classic tradition," a "plain Marxist" and especially an intellectual craftsman who sweated over his prose, which became less academic and more vernacular over time. "Isn't there room for just plain solid stuff; workmanlike stuff by an artisan stratum?" he wondered to his friend Lewis Coser at mid-decade. "That's my ideal kind of production and reception."

Other correspondence records his wide-ranging amateur interests: in music, movies, motorcycles, photography, art and architecture. They indicate an approach to reflection not as the highly technical endeavor so characteristic of the twentieth century but instead as a deeply personal, occasionally aesthetic way of realizing older notions of selfhood in a world now constrained by impersonal institutions. To Dwight Macdonald, Mills defined *White Collar* as a series of "prose poems" toward such a realization. "The book is my little work of art," he wrote elsewhere. And the "politics of truth" which so exercised Mills' evangelical imagination implied "the act of a free man who rejects 'fate;' it is an affirmation of oneself as a moral and intellectual center of responsible decision." Even his idiosyncratic style seemed a response to the sterile rituals of professionalism. He wrote in a 1948 letter, "About flamboyance: don't you love it? God, the only way to live: the only personal answer to bureaucratic precision and form which, part of the managerial demiurge, would stultify everything we do and are."

In a 1956 letter to novelist Harvey Swados, his neighbor and confidant, Mills claimed that "what these jokers—all of them—don't realize is that way down deep and systematically I'm a goddamned anarchist." This best describes his own view of his temperament, at the center of which stood a visceral determination to avoid the "sense of the trap" that he seemed to see around every American corner. The actual substance of his concerns points toward a more traditional conclusion. He opposed promiscuous mingling of Freud and Marx, defended liberal education and promoted a national civil service as well as a "genuine bureaucracy." He defined the "cultural apparatus" as "the seat of civilization," invoking no less an apostle of sensibility than Matthew Arnold. Sending a telegram to a rally against the Bay of Pigs, he rested his case on the most familiar of distinctions: "Kennedy and company have returned us to barbarism."

Mills came to believe that the freedom and reason embedded in "the big discourse" he first learned in Texas would require the

radical subversion of the prevailing order. He concluded that Columbia University belonged to him and his kind. His colleagues
had "defaulted." Others will catalogue other motives for his
ambition, but his letters and autobiographical compositions show
his sense of his role as a redeemer of lost ideals, an old-fashioned
moralist in a time of "mindlessness" and existential despair. That
his public moralism coincided with a flawed personal life did not
escape his sense of irony, nor the attentions of his many academic
enemies.

Mills hoped to belong to "the heritage that mankind has produced in its best moments." His extensive writings to an imaginary
Russian friend, Tovarich, suggest how alone he believed he was
in this aspiration. That so many have flocked to his work in the
past four decades also shows how mistaken that conviction has
become.

THE DECIDERS

The opening sentence of C. Wright Mills' *The Power Elite* might have seemed unremarkable. "The powers of ordinary men are circumscribed by the everyday worlds in which they live, yet even in these rounds of job, family and neighborhood they often seem driven by forces they can neither understand nor govern."

When the book was published in 1956, however, it exploded into a culture riddled with existential anxiety and political fear. Mills—a broad-shouldered, motorcycle-riding anarchist from Texas who taught sociology at Columbia—argued that the "sociological key" to American uneasiness could be found not in the mysteries of the unconscious nor in the battle against Communism, but in the over-organization of society. At the pinnacle of the government, the military and the corporations, a small group of men made the decisions that reverberated "into each and every cranny" of American life. "Insofar as national events are decided," Mills wrote, "the power elite are those who decide them."

The argument met with criticism from all sides. "I look forward to the time when Mr. Mills hands back his prophet's robes and settles down to being a sociologist again," Arthur Schlesinger Jr. wrote in *The New York Post*. Adolf Berle, writing in the *New York Times Book Review*, said that while the book contained "an uncomfortable degree of truth," Mills presented "an angry cartoon, not a serious picture." Liberals could not believe a book about power in America said so little about the Supreme Court, while conservatives attacked it as leftist psychopathology ("sociological mumbo jumbo," *Time* said). The Soviets translated it in 1959, but decided it was pro-American. "Although Mills expresses a skeptical and critical attitude toward bourgeois liberalism and its society of power," said the introduction to the Russian translation, "his hopes and sympathies undoubtedly remain on its side."

The *Power Elite* found an eclectic audience at home and abroad. Fidel Castro and Che Guevara debated the book in the Sierra Maestra. Jean-Paul Sartre and Simone de Beauvoir published excerpts in their radical journal, *Les Temps Modernes*. In the United States, Mills received hundreds of letters from Protestant clergymen, professors and students, pacifists and soldiers. This note came from an Army private stationed in San Francisco: "I genuinely appreciate reading in print ideas I have thought about some time ago. At that time, they seemed to me so different that I didn't tell anyone." In the aftermath of the global riots of 1968, the CIA identified Mills as one of the most influential New Left intellectuals in the world, though he had been dead for six years.

The historical value of *The Power Elite* seems assured. It was the first book to offer a serious model of power that accounted for the secretive agencies of national security. Mills saw the post-ideological "postmodern epoch" (as he would later call it) at its inception, and his book remains a founding text in the continuing demand for democratically responsible political leadership—a demand echoed and amplified across the decades in books like Christopher Lasch's *Revolt of the Elites* (1995), Kevin Phillips' *Wealth and Democracy* (2002), and Chalmers Johnson's *Sorrows of Empire* (2004).

Much of *The Power Elite* was a tough-talking polemic against the "romantic pluralism" embedded in the prevailing theory of American politics. The separation of powers in the Constitution, the story went, repelled the natural tendency of power to concentrate, while political parties and voluntary societies organized the clash of interests, laying the people's representatives open to the influence of public opinion. This "theory of balance" still applied to the "middle levels of power," Mills wrote, but the society it envisioned had been eclipsed. For the first time in history, he argued, the territories of the United States made up a self-conscious mass society. If the economy had once been a multitude of locally or regionally rooted, equal units of production, it now answered to the needs of a few hundred corporations. If the government had once been a patchwork of states held together by Congress, it now answered to the initiatives of a strong executive. If the military had once been a militia system resistant to the discipline of permanent training, it now consumed half the national budget and seated its admirals and generals in the biggest office building in the world.

The "awesome means of power" enthroned upon these monopolies of production, administration and violence included the power to prevent issues and ideas from reaching Congress in the first place. Most Americans still believed the ebb and flow of public opinion guided political affairs. "But now we must recognize this description as a set of images out of a fairy tale," Mills wrote. "They are not adequate even as an approximate model of how the American system of power works."

The small groups of men standing at the head of the three monopolies represented a new kind of elite, one whose character and conduct mirrored the antidemocratic ethos of their institutions. The corporations recruited from the business schools, and conceived executive training programs that demanded strict conformity. The military selected generals and admirals from the service academies, and inculcated "the caste feeling" by segregating them from the associational life of the country. Infrequently did local apprenticeships serve as a passport to the government's executive chambers. Of the appointees in the Eisenhower administration, Mills found that a record number had never stood for election at any level.

Above the apparent balance of powers, Mills said, "an intricate set of overlapping cliques" shared in "decisions having at least national consequences." Rather than operating in secret, the same kinds of men—who traded opinions in the same churches, clubs and schools—took turns in the same jobs. Mills pointed to the personnel traffic among the Pentagon, the White House and the corporations. The nation's three top policy positions—secretary of state, treasury and defense—were occupied by former corporate executives. The president was a general.

Mills could not answer many of the most important questions he raised. How did the power elite make its decisions? Did its members cause their roles to be created, or step into roles already created? Around what interests did they cohere? He asserted a "coincidence of interest" partially organized around "a permanent war establishment," but he did little more than assert it. Most of the time, he said, the power elite did not cohere at all. "This instituted elite is frequently in some tension: it comes together only on certain coinciding points and only on certain occasions of 'crisis'." Although he urged his readers to scrutinize the commanding power of decision, his book did not scrutinize any decisions.

These ambiguities have kept *The Power Elite* vulnerable to the charge of conspiracy-mongering. In an essay in *Playboy*, "Who Rules America?", Arthur Schlesinger Jr. repeated his earlier skepticism about Mills' argument, calling it "a sophisticated version of the American nightmare." Alan Wolfe has pointed out that while Mills got much about the self-enriching ways of the corporate elite right, his vision of complacent American capitalism did not anticipate the competitive dynamics of our global economy. Of late, we have seen that "occasions of crisis" do not necessarily serve to unify the generals with the politicians.

Yet *The Power Elite* abounds with questions that still trouble us today. Can a strong democracy coexist with the amoral ethos of corporate elites? Can public argument have democratic meaning in the age of national security? The trend in foreign affairs, Mills argued, was for a militarized executive branch to bypass the United Nations, while Congress was left with little more than the power to express "general confidence, or the lack of it." Policy tended to be announced as doctrine, which was then sold to the public via the media. Career diplomats in the State Department believed they could not truthfully report intelligence. Meanwhile official secrecy expanded its reach. "For the first time in American history, men in authority are talking about an 'emergency' without a foresee-able end," Mills wrote in a sentence that remains as powerful and unsettling as it was 50 years ago. "Such men as these are crackpot realists: in the name of realism they have constructed a paranoid reality all their own."

NO-MAN'S-LAND:
C. WRIGHT MILLS IN ENGLAND

C
Wright Mills had a little to say about a great many subjects and a lot to say about a few subjects of great importance. *The New Men of Power* (1948), *White Collar* (1951), and *The Power Elite* (1956), his trilogy, marks a fault line in Anglo-American cultural history, not only between the Left, old and new, but also between the modern and the "post-modern epoch," as he wrote in 1959.

Modern ideologies marshaled the Enlightenment against the myth, fraud, and superstition of the medieval epoch. Liberalism and Marxism developed theories of human beings as secular, rational, peaceable creatures, then transformed these theories into collective projects. The social structure of advanced industrial capitalism, however, defeated the ideologies of progress. The failures, betrayals, and ambiguities of liberalism and Marxism disinherited modern man, according to Mills, who wrote as a defender of humanist aspiration as well as a witness to its eclipse.

No biography of Mills worth reading has appeared in the forty-five years since his death. This is surprising. He was a spiritual descendant of Stendhal's Julien Sorel, Turgenev's Bazarov, and Jack London's Martin Eden, one in a long line of "new men" born into mass society. Sons without fathers, non-party revolutionists, they were intellectuals as well as actors, roles between which they acknowledged no need to choose. They stole into the imagination of Europe and America in the nineteenth century and played havoc ever after.

Mills, too, was an outlander. Born in Waco, Texas, in 1916, he endured a year in military school before enrolling in the University of

Texas in 1935. In Austin, he studied sociology and philosophy with a group of professors trained in the Chicago School of pragmatism. At the University of Wisconsin, where he went for his doctorate in sociology and anthropology, he met German social thought in the person of Hans Gerth, the refugee scholar. Following an interlude at the University of Maryland, he joined Columbia College in 1945. He taught there until his death, in 1962.

A Texan by birth, an anarchist by temperament, a pragmatist by training, Mills made himself into a "Hemingway Man." An autobiographical note in 1953 envisioned his breakout from Morningside Heights: "The Hemingway Man is a spectator and an experiencer; he is also a world traveller, usually alone or with changing companions. When I have travelled and camped out west, when I have thought about Europe, always when I have thought about Europe, I have tried in somewhat feeble ways perhaps even ridiculous ways, to be a Hemingway Man."

Mills grew into the role he set for himself as if expanding in concentric circles, first focusing on the American Midwest, then widening to encompass the cities of the East, then radiating outward to Europe, where he went for the first time in 1956. Late though he was in going abroad, he was not long in making up the time. He arrived as the Cold War system in international politics was suffering shocks from which it was never fully to recover. Writing in 1957, after spending a weekend with the Students' Union of the London School of Economics, he saw a possible renaissance in humanist values: "I've the vague feeling that 'we' may be coming into our own in the next five or ten years."

▌▌▌

If 1948 was the last year of the thirties in the United States, let 1956 stand as the first year of the sixties in England. Khrushchev's speech against Stalin collided with the rebellions in Poland and Hungary later in the year to burn away the last residue of faith. Belief in the need for a revolutionary Left now coincided with disbelief in the Communist Party as its organizing agent and moral tutor. E. P. Thompson and John Saville, two of 7,000 who resigned their Party memberships after the events of 1956, founded the *New Reasoner* to educate the disappointed and savage the culpable. Thompson assailed Stalinism as "militant philistinism" and demanded a confrontation with its crimes.

Mills learned about the personalities and politics of the changing English Left from a Belgian Jewish émigré named Ralph Miliband, who had invited him to the LSE. Miliband was a perfect host. A member of the editorial board of the *New Reasoner*, he had joined forces with a second group of dissenters, headquartered at Oxford University. It was the Suez affair, rather than the crisis of communism, that quickened pulses. Awareness that a post-ideological epoch had already dawned was the theme of the Oxford group's magazine, *Universities and Left Review*.

An early contribution to the magazine by Stuart Hall, "A Sense of Classlessness" (1958), located the real significance of the Suez affair at home. A "sense of class confusion" befogged liberal and Marxist efforts to describe post-war English society and its resource-grabbing foreign policy, Hall thought. Urban housing complexes were replacing brick homes in working-class neighborhoods, where attitudes were changing in favor of automobiles, kitchen appliances, and televisions. Corporations were conquering small enterprises with the aid of bureaucracies that were reaching deeper into private life. "A number of interpenetrating elites or narrow oligarchies" now superintended "a permanently exploited, permanently alienated 'mass' of consumers—consuming goods and culture equally. The true class picture which so skillfully conceals itself behind the bland face of contemporary capitalism is broadly speaking that which C. Wright Mills describes in *The Power Elite*."

Mills visited his new friends in England as often as he could. He appeared on *We Dissent*, a television documentary produced by Kenneth Tynan. He headlined a speaker series in Soho at the Partisan Cafe, a forum run by *Universities and Left Review*. He went with Miliband to Warsaw, where he met Zygmunt Bauman, Julian Hochfeld, and Leszek Kolakowski, leaders of Poland's 1956. In the best-selling pamphlet that grew out of the trip, *The Causes of World*

War Three (1958), Mills asked readers to imagine "a world without passports" and argued forcefully for the political independence of Europe.

Around his academic colleagues at Columbia, Mills guarded his manner. Around his friends in England, he let out his gregarious side. "He had this enormous intellectual curiosity, a real willingness to learn," Norman Birnbaum has said. John Saville has "very warm memories" of him: "He was an extremely lively, very intelligent, bloody interesting intellectual." Stuart Hall, Charles Taylor, and Peter Worsley held similar impressions.

Mills arrived in London on Saturday, January 10, 1959, for a week's visit. The next day, he appeared on a television program. On Monday, Tuesday, and Thursday, he delivered the University Lectures in Sociology at the London School of Economics. He found time to attend Miliband's seminar on political theory, fielding questions from the students, and to attend a meeting of the editorial board of the *New Reasoner* at Doris Lessing's flat. Dorothy Thompson, watching him on television, thought he looked like most American professors. Then she met him at Lessing's, "and this great cowboy heaved into sight." In Mills she perceived an example of left-wing integrity, a man of commitment in an age of collapsing faiths: "He was a good listener, and intellectually very curious and open. I was completely swept away."

The BBC recorded Mills' LSE lectures and broadcast them for three weeks. The *Times* described him as "6 ft tall, with a chest like a grizzly-bear's and a face as tanned and craggy as a cowboy's." According to the *Times Literary Supplement*, "Mr. Wright Mills bursts among the pundits' discussion of the American situation with the explosive force of James Cagney at a tea party of the Daughters of the American Revolution." Michael Foot, editor of the weekly *London Tribune*, announced: "HERE, AT LAST, IS THE TRUE VOICE OF AMERICAN RADICALISM." Mills was "radical, adventurous, free of jingoism and militarism, open to exciting thought and effective popular action." Many English intellectuals believed the Cold War had snuffed out America's revolutionary heritage, "but it is not dead. And it speaks through Wright Mills."'

Mills' "Letter to the New Left" summoned these special relations to a consummatory moment. Published in September 1960 in the *New Left Review* (the project of a merger between the *New Reasoner* and *Universities and Left Review*), the letter implored English intellectuals to transform the absence of ideology into new theories of history and human nature, to take what they needed from the warring dogmas of the Cold War and leave the rest behind. Mills wrote in slangy prose and memorable wisecracks, but it was the first paragraph that endeared him to his comrades abroad: "When I settle down to you, I feel somehow 'freer' than usual. The reason, I suppose, is that most of the time I am writing for people whose ambiguities and values I imagine to be rather different from mine; but with you, I feel enough in common to allow us to 'get on with it' in more positive ways."

Getting on with it meant going to Cuba. In August 1960, Mills took two Nikon cameras and an audio recorder out of his suitcase, dropped into a jeep waiting outside the Havana Riviera, and toured the island. Everywhere he looked, he saw a society expanding under a morning sun of success. A revolution had convulsed a despotism. The military stage of the revolution was turning into reconstruction by voluntary self-education. Standing in a downpour at the edge of a former cattle ranch, Mills listened to Fidel Castro and a cadre of military officers debate the best species of tree to plant in the fields. "So the real ideological conflict under discussion is pine trees versus eucalyptus!" he exclaimed into his recorder.

"We are new men," proclaimed *Listen, Yankee* (1960). "That is why we are so original and so spontaneous and so unafraid to do what must be done in Cuba." Mills' pamphlet, part explanation, part evocation, met with unified acrimony in the United States. The *New Republic* compared him to "a merger of Judas Iscariot, Benedict Arnold, and Vidkun Quisling, retaining the worst features of each." The *Washington Post* compared him to Wilhelm Reich, a genius gone mad. Syndicated columnists assailed him in towns and small cities from coast to coast. "Don't Let Prof Mills Fool You on Cuba" ran one headline; "Author of Book on Cuba Thinks He Fools You" ran another. The Federal Bureau of Investigation deployed agents near his home in West Nyack, New York. The strain was too much. The night before Mills was to debate the revolution on NBC television, he suffered a heart attack that put him into a coma. Pushed by hostility at home, pulled by the offer of a chair in sociology at the University of Sussex, he returned to England in April 1961. He took a flat in London, enrolled his daughter in school, and thought about settling.

Meanwhile, the *New Left Review* confronted a crisis. The magazine's ambitious publishing arm had issued a series of pamphlets, but organizational bickering and financial difficulties had impeded progress. E. P. Thompson, broke and demoralized, arrived at editorial meetings with holes in his shoes. Both John Saville, chairman of the magazine, and Stuart Hall, editor from its inception, quit the board late in 1961. Other resignations followed.

The disarray only enhanced Mills' value as a mentor. Perry Anderson and Robin Blackburn, part of the second generation of student radicals to rattle through Oxford, met with him often in these months. "We were pumping him for information and advice," recalls Blackburn, who also remembers looking on, guiltily, as Mills strained to climb the stairs to the fifth-floor flat where they held their tutorials. Cuban politics and classical social theory dominated the sessions. Mills' *The Sociological Imagination* (1959) struck Anderson and Blackburn as a text at once exotic and relevant. Sociology had gained a toehold at the LSE, and the British Sociological Association (BSA) had opened in 1951. But most of the founders of the BSA did not identify themselves as sociologists. Membership still counted in the low hundreds, and only two universities had departments, neither located at Oxford or Cambridge.

"We live in a society that is essentially opaque," wrote Anderson and Blackburn in *New University*, a campus extension of the *New Left Review*. "The origin and sense of the events in it systematically escape us. This obscurity is also a separation: it prevents us seeing one another and our common situations as they really are, and so divide us from each other." Along came Mills, promising that sociology, classically conceived, could uncover orienting points and organizing principles, could spur "a transvaluation of values." His radically sociological approach to power offered methodological aid as well. In 1957, a group of researchers for *Universities and Left Review* compiled the income, benefits, training, and social connections of the men who staffed the top posts in industry. The group titled its report *The Insiders* (1957) after determining that a few hundred corporations controlled the economy, and that wherever the state intervened, it became a partner in monopoly enterprise rather than its critic. "Public ownership," the slogan of state socialism, masked oligarchy. *Universities and Left Review* published *The Insiders* as a pamphlet, which sold out quickly.

No record remains of Mills' impressions of Anderson and Blackburn, but they must have impressed him strongly. One of the last things he did in January 1962, when he went home to die, was to nominate a new editor for the *New Left Review*. Anderson assumed control and Blackburn joined the editorial board in March, the month Mills succumbed to a heart attack. He was forty-five.

███

E. P. Thompson compared Mills to William Morris. "We had come to assume his presence—definitions, provocations, exhortations—as a fixed point in the intellectual night-sky," Thompson wrote in a two-part essay on Mills in *Peace News*: "His star stood above the ideological no-man's land between the orthodox emplacements of West and East, flashing urgent humanist messages. If we couldn't always follow it, we always stopped to take bearings." Ralph Miliband mourned his death "bitterly and personally" in the *New Left Review*: "In a trapped and inhumane world, he taught what it means to be a free and humane intellect." Miliband named his newborn son after him in 1965. "1 got to feel closer to Mills than I have ever felt to any man, or shall ever feel again, I should think," Miliband wrote to Thompson.

The editorial reconstitution of *New Left Review* instilled in veterans of *Universities and Left Review* and the *New Reasoner* "a sense of isolation," Thompson later wrote. Those who had come to political awareness in the thirties and forties, for whom 1956 had been a pivotal year, lost the initiative to a generation that came to awareness in the late fifties. As a Labour government assumed power in 1964 and supported the American war in Vietnam, it was Anderson and Blackburn who directed the New Left in England.

Mills' influence continued. Blackburn's long essay and most important early work, "Prologue to the Cuban Revolution" (1963), offered a sociological history of the "power structure" in Cuba and a political alternative to the liberal portrait of a middle-class revolution betrayed. According to Blackburn, Cuba's belated independence from Spain, the shocks delivered to its economic and political institutions in the decades thereafter, plus foreign manipulation of its markets: these peculiarities of Cuban history had inhibited social cohesion on the island. The middle-class had not developed any collective interests, had not grown conscious of itself as an ideological opponent of Fulgencio Batista's dictatorship. Rather than standing for any popular goals or social programs, Batista had ruled through a patchwork of strategic alliances, the hollowness of which was revealed by its inability to sustain a fight against the outnumbered, outgunned guerrillas. These weaknesses of ideology and social structure explained why the dictatorship had collapsed so speedily, leaving behind a vacuum. Castro's guerrillas, once in power, expanded into it with a comprehensive program of practical assistance.

Anderson's "Origins of the Present Crisis" (1965) and "Components of the National Culture" (1968) worked the theoretical side of his inheritance into a paradox: England, the cradle of capitalism, had produced neither first-class Marxist theoreticians nor bourgeois sociologists equivalent to French and German exemplars. In Anderson's struggle to see through this background of parochial complacency, in his effort to gain a total view of social structure by means of a sociological analysis that was at once historical and comparative, the hidden hand of Mills showed through.

Mills lived on as political ally, as sociological tutor, and as the author of aphorisms, epigrams, and slogans that lingered and expanded in the minds of his English readers. Labour MP Anthony Crosland complained to the BBC about the diffusion of his ideas: "Many people on the left see America as the arch-capitalist country dominated by a power elite of big industrialists, Wall Street bankers, military men and all the rest of it. And so, since they are anticapitalist, they are inevitably anti-American. Personally, I think that this picture of America is terribly exaggerated. I do not think America is run in this crude way by a capitalistic power elite." An essay by Denis Brogan in the *Times Literary Supplement*, titled "Spooks of the Power Elite," also complained about his influence. Mills "appeals to the same conspiratorial tastes on the left as do the theories of the John Birch Society on the right. His diagnosis is fundamentally passive and pessimistic." His admirers, however, did not fail to recognize the positive intentions behind his post-1956 work, his effort to forge from the homelessness of radical values a new beginning. They remembered, all too well, what he had said of those values in his LSE lectures in 1959: "It is time for us to try to realize them ourselves—in our own lives, in our own direct action, in the immediate context of our own work. Now, we ought to repossess our cultural apparatus and use it for our own purposes."

∎∎∎

In October 1966, the Socialist Society at the LSE published a pamphlet challenging the selection of Walter Adams as the school's new director. The pamphlet argued that Adams, recently the Principal of University College in Rhodesia, had not proved himself liberal enough on the matter of race to enjoy the privilege of leading a student body riddled with questions about colonialism. The pamphlet struck up a furor. The leader of the LSE Students' Union sought answers about the appointment from the official selection committee. Instead, he was arraigned by a disciplinary court for criticizing school authorities—an offense against regulations. Very soon, protest over the new director grew into the first major student strike in English history.

The rebellion at the LSE introduced sit-ins, boycotts, and marches that lasted for the remainder of the academic year. Here as elsewhere, not only the decisions of the authorities, but the authority to make the decisions stimulated the indignation of students. Officials punished them for defying the rituals of dissent. The punishments spurred bolder acts of defiance. Most English universities endured such conflicts in the sixties, but none rivaled the LSE for scale. More than 40 percent of the student population took part in at least one of the protests in 1966 and 1967; more than 60 percent of sociology students did so. And here as elsewhere, the confrontation escalated in 1968. Thousands of protesters were expected to come to London at the end of October to voice their displeasure over the war in Vietnam. Would the LSE allow some of them to stay on campus? Walter Adams would not. Eight hundred students seized a building for themselves.

Robin Blackburn, recently appointed lecturer in sociology at the LSE, co-edited a volume of essays on the occupation: *Student Power* (1969). The essays connected the state of production and consumption in advanced capitalism to the misshapen condition of higher education and challenged the image of universities as island communities, innocent of the violence of foreign policy. As Perry Anderson wrote in his contribution, "This is a direct attack on the reactionary and mystifying culture inculcated in universities and colleges, and which it is one of the fundamental purposes of British higher education to instill in students."

References to Mills appeared throughout *Student Power*, but the essays, ironically, bore the greater influence of French, German, and Italian Marxists. The irony lay in the ideology. Mills had made his appeal in England as a critic of left-wing cant and dogma. Alone among American intellectuals, he brought none of the moral liabilities of a communist past and at the same time exemplified unbroken radical commitment. This effort to stand in no-man's-land, taking fire from both sides, made his work uniquely available to dissenters on all sides of the Cold War. His greatest achievement was his independence. "There is now no substantial reason to believe that Marxist revolutions will come about in any foreseeable future in any major advanced capitalist country," he wrote in 1962, completing the end-of-ideology thesis in his trilogy.

The movement for an independent Left in England, thus encouraged, had been born in its refusal to be misled by the false rivalry of communist and bourgeois. It had withdrawn from the bankrupted ideologies of the modern period so as to begin the task of rehabilitating the moral culture of humanism. Yet when the most important student strike in English history presented itself, the New Left imported its model of thinking from a knock-off edition of the same old texts.

▌▌▌

Anderson's paradox, bemoaning the apparent fact that England had given birth to the social system of capitalism without producing any corresponding Marxist thinkers, was an actual paradox only from the perspective of the Marxist theory of history. "The starting point here," Anderson wrote, "will be any observed irregularities in the contours of British culture, viewed internationally. That is, any basic phenomena which are not a matter of course, but contradict elementary expectation from comparative experience and hence seem to demand a special explanation. Such irregularities may provide a privileged point of entry into the culture as a whole, and thereby furnish a key to the system." Or, in other words, Anderson slipped on X-ray glasses, which afforded him metaphysical confidence that "the system" could be rendered transparent. Then, looking through his "privileged points of entry into the system," he identified the very asymmetries, irregularities, and disjunctions Marxism had keyed him to find in the first place. The bourgeois opposition he buried in overlapping contexts. His own model he floated above time and place: "Marx's thought was so far in advance of its time and its society that it was unassimilable in the nineteenth century."

Mills had called such reasoning by fiat "Sophisticated Marxism" and likened its obfuscating function to Grand Theory in liberal social thought. In both cases, he wrote, a "sophisticated" conceptual knowledge and elaboration of radical theory coincided with a radically arrant political intelligence; what appeared to be a bid for greater rationalism concealed a note of mysticism. As Anderson wrote, in a characteristic tautology: "Events that fail to happen are often more important than those which do; but they are always infinitely more difficult to see."

If Anderson was right about "the complete mutism of the past" and the "objective vacuum at the centre of the culture," did this mean there was nothing in society to defend? Blackburn's contribution to

Student Power gave a clear answer. "A Brief Guide to Bourgeois Ideology" said Anglo-American social theory was nothing more than the functions it fulfilled in "the system," the wheels and levers, pulleys and pumps, hooks and handles of the capitalist machine. Ideas? No more than myths by which the "power elite" ruled. Blackburn hooted at "bourgeois analysts," "the bourgeois political theorist," "bourgeois social theory," "bourgeois economists," "bourgeois sociologists," "the myths of bourgeois pluralism," "most bourgeois theorists," "the customary refuge of the bourgeois sociologist," "the weak stomach of the modern bourgeois social theorist," "the amnesia of modern bourgeois epigones," and on and on. Subtracting the word "bourgeois" from the essay would have exposed it as a mix of phrase-mongering and finger-pointing.

The New Left gained something more decisive than polemical firepower from its turn toward Marxism. Anderson made much of the fact that both Marxism and bourgeois sociology had produced a "theory of society as a totality," arguing that without such a concept of totality, then "the era of revolutions is, necessarily, unthinkable." It was this longing for a concept of totality, needed for the purposes of clarification and available in Marx's metaphysics, that struck Anderson and Blackburn blind when they went to judge the political significance of the occupation of the LSE.

The manifesto of the Revolutionary Socialist Students' Federation told the tale. Adopted in November 1968 and subsequently published in the *New Left Review*, the manifesto shunted aside political parties, trade unions, and student reform organizations. "Mass democracy," it said, required "red bases in our colleges and universities" on the model pioneered by Mao Tse-tung's Cultural Revolution. Here was a concept of totality armed and dangerous. Begun in 1966 under the banner "Combat Bourgeois ideas," Mao's program was in the hands of Chinese students, who were burning books, closing parks, destroying paintings, and torturing their teachers. "It should not be thought that the call to make the creation of Red Bases a strategic goal of our struggle is merely a flight of rhetoric," Blackburn explained, in the same issue of the magazine that carried the RSSF's manifesto: "Capitalist power cannot just be drowned in a rising tide of consciousness. It must be smashed and broken up by the hard blows of popular force."

Communications from Mao appeared in the *New Left Review* alongside enthusiastic reports from the Cultural Revolution. When Anderson wrote an introduction to Marshall Mikhail Tukhachevsky, it was not difficult to share his preference for Mao. It ought to have been difficult to credit the comparison in the first place, morally thin as the choices were. Observe that Anderson believed Mao's theory of revolutionary practice was driving war and politics into a new unity. Recall how the Chinese students were treating their teachers. Now listen to Anderson on the occupation of the LSE: "A revolutionary culture is not for tomorrow. But a revolutionary practice within culture is possible and necessary today. The student struggle is its initial form."

On the evening of 24 January 1969, Blackburn was presenting a paper to a conference of the British Sociological Association. Gathered on the fourth floor of the St. Clement's building at the LSE, the conferees heard shouting through the window. A young man bounded into the room and interrupted Blackburn's presentation. While you are talking about the revolution, said the young man, it is happening outside. LSE officials had installed iron gates to guard against breaches of security. An emergency meeting of the Students' Union had threatened to rip them down. Now a crowd of students tugged and whacked at the gates with a sledgehammer, crowbars, and pickaxes. They went at it for about an hour.

Later that night, in a previously scheduled speech, Blackburn celebrated the attack on the gates. Had he fallen silent then, rather than repeating his remarks on BBC television on January 30th, he might have evaded punishment. Instead, he was instructed to appear before a disciplinary tribunal, which was empowered to reconsider his future at the school. His letter of reply jeered at "the entire clique of self-appointed capitalist manipulators."

The "capitalist manipulators" acknowledged that Blackburn had neither committed any direct actions nor incited any. He had made his remarks after the gates had fallen. They fired him anyway and closed the LSE for twenty-five days. The Maoists responded by occupying a building at the University of London and setting up an LSE-in-Exile. They greeted the reopening of the LSE a month later by boycotting classes, interrupting lectures, tossing stink bombs into meetings, and pulling fire alarms.

The LSE-in-Exile closed one day after it opened. The Revolutionary Socialist Students' Federation folded. By the end of the summer of 1969, scarcely a year after Anderson made his revolutionary prophecy, the rebellion at the LSE stammered and wheezed to a halt. Thereafter, student interest in sociology fell, while the "capitalist manipulators" moved on to other enemies: inflation, shrinking support from the state, and dwindling morale. The American war in Asia went on and on.

▪▪▪

What would Mills have thought? In 1959 at the LSE, he recommended "direct action." The next year, his "Letter to the New Left" exhorted the uncorrupted to consider that "the cultural apparatus, the intellectuals" might be best positioned to initiate a new beginning. He lectured on the subject in Austria, Brazil, Canada, Cuba, Denmark, Mexico, Poland, West Germany, and the Soviet Union. By and by, he spread his message all over the world. In September 1968, the Central Intelligence Agency concluded a classified report, "Restless Youth," which identified Herbert Marcuse, Mills, and Frantz Fanon as the three leaders of the international Left. Between Marcuse's abstract Marxism and Fanon's revolutionary violence, there was his ghost, chasing both action and ideas without acknowledging the need to choose.

The New Man's dream of creating new values out of the dialectic of thought and action must always know the difference between thinking too long and acting too soon. Mills' American followers, no better at telling this vital difference than their English counterparts, met the same end. With the LSE strike about to break out, Columbia University students took over Hamilton Hall, the building where Mills had once had his office. Four additional buildings fell in quick succession. *Who Rules Columbia?* a pamphlet written by his former students on the model of *The Insiders,* justified the occupation, after which a Strike Education Committee opened a "Liberation School" that lasted not much longer than the LSE-in-Exile. Tom Hayden, an ardent admirer of Mills, presided for four days in Mathematics Hall, where he showed teams of militants how to slick the steps with soap in preparation for the police. "Columbia opened a new tactical stage in the resistance movement which began last fall," Hayden wrote after the bust, sounding like Perry Anderson. "What is certain is that we are moving toward power—the power to stop the machine if it cannot be made to serve humane ends," he wrote, in the same vein of misbegotten prophecy.

As Mills' students carried his writings from 1956 into the maelstrom of 1968, the meaning of his biography changed in response to events he could not have been expected to anticipate. He may have accepted his portion of responsibility for the psychodynamics of the international Left before it reorganized into terrorist cells. Had he lived long enough to choose sides in 1968, however, his experimentalism would have seen him through many unknown contingencies, which would have altered and improved his perspective many times by then. All along, his pragmatism would have tempered his exhortations. The "Letter to the New Left" reminded readers to be "realistic in our utopianism" and asked: "Is anything more certain than that in 1970 our situation will be quite different?" Most likely, the choice of sides would not have been his to make. In his independence, he had refused to narrow the idea of radical commitment to a choice between confrontation and withdrawal. Yet these were the only terms on offer from his enemies and epigones at the end of the decade. His legacy torn apart by the very forces he unleashed, he would have been marooned on no-man's-land.

The full story of Mills' life and thought, cast across three generations of intellectuals on four continents, stands uniquely at the intersection of history and biography, illuminating the incidents, sentiments, and personalities of the international Left. If that sounds trite, think of the anniversary of '68 upon us; of the leftward surge in Latin America; of the unpopular war in Iraq, waged by American elites with the support of a Labour government—and linger on the news that David Wright Miliband is Foreign Secretary. Set against the possibilities for *another beginning,* the untold tales of Mills' life and thought may yet reveal how the New Men turned into Hemingway Men, how Hemingway Men became Castro's Men, and how Castro's Men became Mao's Men before the rest of us became…Academic Men.

THE EPIGONE'S EMBRACE:
IRVING LOUIS HOROWITZ ON
C. WRIGHT MILLS

I rving Louis Horowitz visited Yaroslava Mills in West Nyack, New
York, soon after she became a widow. He greeted her as a friend
and colleague of her late husband, C. Wright Mills. Before he
left that spring afternoon, in 1962, he borrowed an unnoticed num-
ber of cartons containing an unknown quantity of Mills' papers. In
June, he finished writing an introduction to forty-one of the essays.
In July, in an obituary notice in the American Journal of Sociology,
he hailed Mills as a spiritual descendent of Voltaire and Diderot. In
August, *Power, Politics, and People: The Collected Essays of C. Wright
Mills*, edited by Irving Louis Horowitz, was ready to go.

Horowitz had waited two years for his chance. In March 1960,
he had approached the man himself with the idea of editing a volume
of essays in his honor. Mills wrote to his literary agent about the
idea, before (apparently) deciding against it. He was too young, he
explained to Horowitz, "and certainly haven't done enough to warrant such a volume. Nobody has in our generation, or the previous
one." Horowitz, undeterred, wrote to Yaroslava Mills on March 22,
two days after the tragedy. Nineteen days later he wrote to her again.
This time he boasted of his efforts to honor her husband's memory
and offered his personal services for anything that she may need,
"anything from flat tires to zebra hunting to transporting widows
across state lines."

Power, Politics, and People appeared in 1963. It was only the
beginning. In the decade ahead, Horowitz took Mills' legacy firmly

in hand, disseminating his ideas, rebuffing his critics, managing his public image at the time of his greatest significance and popularity. One year after *Power, Politics, and People,* he realized the original idea for a commemorative volume as *The New Sociology: Essays in Social Science and Social Theory in Honor of C. Wright Mills* (1964). That same year, he edited and published Mills' dissertation as *Sociology and Pragmatism: The Higher Learning in America* (1964). Two years later, he had it published again, with a bigger press.

While editing volumes from Mills, Horowitz surrounded them with articles about him. He contributed to *The American Scholar, Studies on the Left, Philosophy and Phenomenological Research,* and other journals of opinion and research. In 1964, he served as chairman of the first selection committee of the "C. Wright Mills Award," which had been inaugurated two years earlier by the Society for the Study of Social Problems. In 1969, he published a second collection of Mills' essays in Mexico City, published in Spanish: *De Hombres Sociales y Movimientos Politicos.* Nobody did more.

■■■

"What was the 'magic' which C. Wright Mills possessed? How did he become the singular intellectual 'hero' of our age?" The opening lines of *Power, Politics, and People* called upon the utopian spirit of the early sixties to recognize "the greatest sociologist the United States has ever produced." Mills had proven uncommonly courageous, conscientious, intelligent, and noble—a political leader who "eschewed the kind of romantic historicism and providential messianism that so often characterizes the truth-seeker"; a scholar who "never confused the art of intellect with the enterprise of making money or getting promoted"; and a public intellectual "tough-minded enough to face the changing world situation and generous enough to recognize that such changes as are brought about are man made." Here had lived a man superabundant with humanity, "an understandable as well as understanding person in his own right." Mills had been one of the "truly great," fit to be mentioned in the company of Marx, Luther, and Socrates.

From the first, Horowitz played fast and loose with facts. The first line of the obituary he wrote for the *American Journal of*

Sociology misstated Mills' age at the time of his death. The preface to
The New Sociology misstated the date of his death. In the introduction
to *Power, Politics, and People,* Horowitz stated that Mills had finished
his Columbia career as associate professor. In fact, Columbia College
had promoted him to full professor on July 1, 1956, a month before
he turned forty. This information anybody could have discovered by
consulting his appointment card at Columbia, or even his entry in
Who's Who in America.

"What do you suppose is going on here?" asked Robert Merton,
in a letter to sociologist William J. Goode on October 22, 1970.
Merton's curiosity was provoked by Alvin Gouldner's *The Coming
Crisis of Western Sociology,* a tract which turned Horowitz's error into
a moral about success in the academy. "Is this merely unbelievably
sloppy 'scholarship'," Merton asked Goode, "or do you think that
ideological commitments are really producing fantasies in the guise
of 'facts'?" A little of both, surely.

The errors, slight in themselves, marred the introductory character of Horowitz's enterprise. The mistakes in the annotations for *De
Hombres Sociales y Movimientos Politicos* must have thrown innumer-
able Mexican intellectuals off the trail. Other blocks of "non-facts"
(as Merton called them) betrayed a definite ideological character.
"With the exception of his election to Phi Beta Kappa, he did not
participate in any of the usual extra-curricular college activities,"
Horowitz declared in the introduction to *Power, Politics, and People,*
in spite of the fact that Mills had served, reluctantly but definitely,
as president of his college's sociological society.

As chairman of the award committee for the Society for the
Study of Social Problems, Horowitz reported the circumstances of
Mills' election to Phi Beta Kappa. "The anomaly of the C. Wright
Mills Award is that Mills himself never received such an award during his lifetime. He was elected to Phi Beta Kappa, but chose not
to accept on the grounds that the Phi Beta Kappa principles foster
elitist orientations in education. Twenty years later he finally chose
to accept this award." That Mills had accepted his Phi Beta Kappa
election in college was recorded on his college transcript and on

every copy of his curriculum vita, as it was recorded by Horowitz's introduction to *Power, Politics, and People*. How or why he came up with the idea that Mills had accepted the award "twenty years later" was impossible to say.

Impossible, literally, because Horowitz did not offer much evidence for such contentions, and because most of the evidence to which he did point was laid away in letters and manuscripts privately held, unavailable to scholars and thus impossible to falsify in accordance with the ethical imperative of independent inquiry. The publication of *Power, Politics, and People*, *The New Sociology*, *Sociology and Pragmatism*, and *De Hombres Sociales y Movimientos Politicos* afforded him a first-run monopoly on Mills. He made ample use of all the rights and privileges assumed by the editorial function, composing prefaces, introductions, and bibliographies, each of them renewing his own invitation to interpret and comment. "The Unfinished Writings of C. Wright Mills," a 1963 article, drew from an unpublished journal of Mills' trip to the Soviet Union. The introduction to *The New Sociology* quoted extensively from unpublished manuscripts Mills had written toward a multivolume work on comparative sociology. Of the twenty-nine essays in the Mexico City collection, half had not been included in *Power, Politics, and People*. Most had never been published during Mills' life. Many are still not available in English.

Horowitz secured his authority by circulating the impression that his work sprung directly out of the special access it had been his privilege to enjoy with the deceased. Here his advantage would have appeared to challengers to be insuperable. He dedicated *Power, Politics, and People* "to Yara," the informal rendering of the name of Mills' widow. The subtitle, "The Collected Essays," gave readers no reason to suspect that not all of Mills' essays were actually collected therein. The preface referred, vaguely, to "my own small role in Wright's achievement."

The New Sociology he ascribed to a gift of grace: "I never saw Mills in a more amenable and relaxed state than that autumn day," Horowitz wrote in the preface. "He was genuinely enthusiastic about the possibilities of such a volume although he continued to harbor misgivings." Here again, the jargon of authenticity, so noticeable in the public speech of the early sixties, bespoke the promotion of a guru. In the preface to *De Hombres Sociales y Movimientos Politicos* he said, "I assure the reader that this represents an authentic work of Mills." The introduction to *Power, Politics, and People* promised to reveal "the 'secret' of Mills' extraordinary ability to communicate with professional and popular audiences alike." Until now, his dissertation had been "shrouded in mystery." Horowitz issued his own personal certificate of authenticity in the preface: "Thus, aside from the rather standard editorial services any good book deserves, the reader can rest assured that this is an authentic and accurately transcribed book of Mills."

Had Mills really wanted his dissertation to be published? "Wright Mills wanted *Sociology and Pragmatism* to be published. In spare moments, he would go over the manuscript for purposes of style and formulation. As a matter of fact, he had submitted the dissertation to various commercial publishers, but no arrangements were arrived at which could prove mutually satisfactory." Had Mills really wanted his dissertation to be published in this format? Henry David Aiken, writing in the *New York Review of Books*, pointed out that Horowitz himself confessed in the preface to having changed the title of the dissertation to *Sociology and Pragmatism: A Study in American Higher Learning.* Actually, Aiken pointed out, Horowitz had titled the dissertation *Sociology and Pragmatism: The Higher Learning in America.* Horowitz, in his reply, said that he had cleaned up the grammar and had inserted chapter headings. He had searched with Mills for the current title. Which title, he did not say.

▌▌▌

If Irving Horowitz had known C. Wright Mills intimately enough to speak for him as well as about him, then why did he commit so many basic biographical errors? In discussing the matter of the honorary volume with Carl Brandt, his agent, in October 1960, Mills seemed to suggest that he had never met, or at least did not remember meeting, his would-be editor. "Horowitz seems like a nice academic type" was the most he mustered in the way of description. It is probable that additional letters, if made public, will fill out the picture of relations between Horowitz and Mills. Nonetheless, Mills lived only fourteen months after writing to Brandt, mostly in Britain, France, Poland, Switzerland, and the Soviet Union, and nowhere in his surviving letters did he nominate an heir, or provide for such broad editorial discretion as Horowitz exercised after his death. Could he have supposed that scholars and writers soon would mistake Horowitz as the executor of his literary estate?

Could he have foretold his posthumous role as benefactor? Horowitz, like him, showed a young talent for noun-heavy sentences overpopulated by polysyllables and mixed metaphors, though Horowitz had a weakness for tautology all his own. In one essay, "Mind, Methodology, and Macrosociology," he explained that "Intellectually, I aim to integrate in my work what is implied precisely by that word itself, namely, intellectuality." This gem he used in the introduction to *Power, Politics, and People*, as well as in other publications, to explain Mills' cultural significance: "He attempted to fuse a liberal imagination with a sociological leavening, and through such a fusion to revive the sinews of democratic politics in America."

Horowitz enjoyed a rapid rise in academic sociology. He signed up with Carl Brandt, Mills' agent. He cultivated relations with Oxford University Press, Mills' publisher. Horowitz, too, served as sociology advisor for Oxford, which published *Power, Politics, and People*, *The New Sociology*, and (the second edition of) *Sociology and Pragmatism*. In virtually everything else he published in the sixties he went out of his way to mention his connection to Mills. His introduction to *The Anarchists* (1964) claimed that "as long ago as 1950, C. Wright Mills was interested in preparing a reader on 'Anarchists, Criminals, and Deviants.'" His book, *Professing Sociology* (1968), relayed opinions that Mills ostensibly held about his major work of social theory, *Character and Social Structure*.

"Irving Louis Horowitz first came to the attention of sociologists as the putative heir of C. Wright Mills," Lewis Coser wrote in a review of Horowitz's *Foundations of Political Sociology* (1972). "On the evidence of this book one is forced to conclude that the inheritance was wholly presumptive." Coser, a longtime friend of Mills, ridiculed Horowitz as a writer of "nonsense" and "anti-meaning," an obfuscator who "isn't just sloppy, he is perversely sloppy." Coser was not alone. Hans Gerth, another longtime friend, denounced him to Yaroslava Mills as "an ignorant young man who unscrupulously pokes with long poles in dark clouds without much luck." Gerth complained that Horowitz was publishing "without regard to truthfulness or accuracy" and telling "little white lies." E.P. Thompson argued that Mills would have objected to the editing and organizing of *Power, Politics, and People*, which was repetitive, ahistorical, and chronologically confused. "Jumbled together in this way," Thompson added, "these essays convey at times the wholly misleading impression of a man of snap judgments and of rhetorical exhortation."

Mills' enemies saw in Horowitz's work unwitting evidence for their own side. Edward Shils thought the introduction to *Power, Politics, and People* was "interesting only for its illustration of the widespread Schwarmerei for Mills' fictitious 'heroism.'" Irving Howe said, "The sad truth is that he deserved the admirers he won: perhaps he even deserved to have Mr. Horowitz edit his book of essays."

Relations between Horowitz and Yaroslava Mills degenerated over the decade. During the spring and summer of 1962, when he won her cooperation, an extraordinary number of responsibilities had befallen her as a result of her husband's sudden death. Her correspondence shows that she had to negotiate his debts, secure his pension, settle the custody of his youngest daughter, resolve a lawsuit against him, select and design his tombstone, console his parents and friends, find a job, and search for childcare, all of this, moreover, while fighting off loneliness and grief.

At first, she gave Horowitz high marks for his editorial energy. But "The Style and Substance of C. Wright Mills," the introduction he wrote for *De Hombres Sociales y Movimientos Politicos*, marked the occasion for a permanent break. Citing a raft of errors and fatuous commentary, she granted permission for the volume on the condition that the introduction not appear with it. She was so upset upon discovering that her veto had been ignored that she refused to grant him permission to publish the essays in an English-language version that Oxford wanted. When Horowitz learned that she was considering publishing the essays with another editor, he threatened to seek a court injunction to stop her. He also threatened to release the English-language version of *De Hombres Sociales y Movimientos Politicos* in advance of her plans, thereby flooding the market. Whatever else happened, he added, he would never yield. Nor would he share his booty, refusing to allow rival biographer Richard Gillam to read the papers, suggesting instead that Gillam purchase a copy of the Spanish-language translations.

By all indications Horowitz came to believe that the papers he had removed from West Nyack belonged to him. In a letter dated May 19, 1964, he acknowledged Yaroslava Mills' desire to have them returned to her possession, and promised that he would do so. And yet five years later, in the middle of the dispute over *De Hombres Sociales y Movimientos Politicos*, she wondered, "How does ILH happen to have this material?" and demanded, in a note addressed to Brandt, "Will he please return all CWM material." Elsewhere, a much different impression set in place. Internal memoranda at Oxford described Horowitz as "a close associate" of Mills, and as "one of his most brilliant students." *Time* magazine ran a feature on the "The New Sociology" in 1970 and chose Horowitz as its exemplary figure in the behavioral sciences. The profile observed that his career "owes much to the late C. Wright Mills." One passage betrayed the character of the obligation: "Horowitz has become executor of Mills' literary estate and the most ferocious advocate of Mills' central thesis: that human society is characterized not by stasis but by radical change." First, a non-fact, followed by a non-idea, and forward went the transformation of a man into a marketable abstraction. In 1972, Horowitz slipped into *Foundations of Political Sociology* the following citation: Horowitz, I.L., ed. (1963) *Power, Politics, and People*, New York, Oxford University Press. Mills' name now failed to appear on his own volume of essays.

"The New Sociology" was an ideologically flexible, philosophically pragmatic, politically liberal form of inquiry that was fashionable for a while in the sixties and seventies. Aspiring to greater intra-vocational cooperation between the social scientists and the social workers of the welfare state, it stressed the practical uses of knowledge put to the improvement of public policy. "This volume celebrates the maturation of classical sociological theory into a crystallized scientific position—stripped of inherited ideological and metaphysical pretenses," Horowitz wrote in the introduction to *The New Sociology*. He showcased what the new sociology could do in the magazine *Trans-action* (founded in 1963 at Washington University), which ran advertisements for his Mills books, and in edited volumes such as *The Rise and Fall of Project Camelot* (1967). In *The War Game* (1963), he criticized the defense intellectuals not for their debased political morality, but for the "logical paradoxes" dogging their war games model. He made "a plea for sharper logical and linguistic distinctions," for "better science—science for survival."

In order to make Mills serve these professional aims, Horowitz represented him as a "true reformer," bleached him of aestheticism, and purged him of utopian yearnings. Oxford's in-house description of *Power, Politics, and People* noted with approval that the selections excluded the sort of polemical material that had appeared in Mills' pamphlets, *The Causes of World War Three* (1958) and *Listen, Yankee* (1960). Mills, according to Horowitz, offered a serviceable sociological equivalent to Walter Lippmann's "public philosophy." In the introduction to *Power, Politics, and People*, he assured his fellow sociologists that "Mills did not make an appeal to partisan passions." On this point he insisted. "What is indisputably clear," he wrote in the *American Journal of Sociology*, "is that Mills never ceased being a sociologist." What about the extraordinary number and variety of disputes that littered his academic career? All of them were explicable in terms of his virtues. "What antagonized many was his singular capacity to transcend the parochialism, the pseudosecularization, and vicious circularity characteristic of the 'peer groups' in American social science." In attacking methodological orthodoxy Mills had identified and filled "a desperate need of the profession," Horowitz explained in *The New Sociology*. "But officialdom was not quite prepared to receive a dark prophet who was willing to take risks by working in areas abandoned by the leading professionals."

In a forty-six page pamphlet, C. *Wright Mills's White Collar* (1967), Horowitz demonstrated how Mills' social thought could be rationalized and made to serve the commercial aspirations of the educational bureaucracy. After summarizing the book in a neutral tone, he gave a desultory "Critical Appraisal," ticked off nine "Suggested Study Topics," and concluded with a section of "Biographical Information" that dragged in errors from his other writings. Published by the R.D.M. Corporation in its "Study Master" series, the pamphlet was marketed to the one group of students least likely to learn anything from it, namely, those who could not be bothered to read *White Collar* for themselves. In 1969, Horowitz tried to put to rest the question of Mills' suitability for the academic life: "I venture to say that when the shouting dies down, as it now largely has abated, Mills will be remembered as a man who uniquely stressed moral purpose in sociology. It was a moral purpose which somehow managed not to intrude on scientific canons but, rather, underscored the scientific enterprise. It did this by showing how sociology as science is a struggle no less than a tradition." Divested, in all these ways, of any particular moral or political commitments, Mills was escorted to his reserved office in the bustling society of academic men.

This was not the only possible interpretation. In London, New York, Prague, Paris, and Warsaw, the rebellions of 1968 climaxed against the background of Mills' biography, and carried forward contentions first aired in his writings: that advanced industrial societies could not be presumed to rest on moral or political consensus; that the achievements of these "overdeveloped" societies rested on the threat of violence, and so taxed the most sensitive and intelligent of their young minds; that the Cold War waged in their name generated psychopathologies overripe for satire and ridicule; that the structure of consent could not easily be altered by the formal mechanics of government.

Mills foresaw, moreover, that the rebellion would originate not in the factories, but in the universities. His "Letter to the New Left," urged the uncorrupted generation to kick the "labor metaphysic," to consider that "the cultural apparatus, the intellectuals," may be best positioned to subvert the social order. Eight years later, after the crises of 1968 shuttered universities around the globe, dissolving tradition, order, and ceremony, setting student against student, professor against professor, the Central Intelligence Agency commissioned a classified report, "Restless Youth." It identified Mills, Herbert Marcuse, and Frantz Fanon as the three most influential leaders of the international Left.

While Horowitz told his peers that Mills belonged in the academy and assured them that he had not appealed to partisan passions, the young intellectuals in Students for a Democratic Society read him as a "radical nomad," and applauded him for his partisan passions. While Horowitz aligned him with the tradition of liberal reform, SDS intellectuals employed his distinction between "reasoning" (a sign of mental activity) and "reasonableness" (a sign of acquiescence) to remind themselves of the differences between radicalism and liberalism. Each side was alive to the pragmatic and democratic content of his thought, but each drew its own conclusion. Horowitz set Mills' sociology to improving public administration. SDS intellectuals set it to direct action and mass protest. Horowitz wrote of "The Stalinization of Fidel Castro." They made a dogma of hombres nuevos.

Horowitz painted them in the worst possible light. The 1968 preface to his *Radicalism and the Revolt Against Reason* (1961) attacked the New Left with arguments first forged by Philip Rieff, Daniel Bell, and Irving Howe, Mills' most ardent critics. The New Left (in this view) did not herald the latent contradictions or paradoxes of postwar capitalism, but gorged itself on genuine ideological and material success. Prosperity and stability had deprived the old left of class analysis, so the new emerged bearing myths and legends about itself and its society. Rejecting parties and organizations, its social analysis quickly degenerated into conspiracy, while its political theory made a fetish of the history-making powers of personal will. According to Horowitz, the New Left's guerrilla phase showed that charismatic gestures already took the place of tangible goals. In the savagery of their passion against "the objectivity of history," the New Leftists found their therapy, but not their solace. Their deviant, irrational conduct would consume them, breeding ever newer waves of revolutionaries dedicated to the purification of their personalities in public action. Seeking salvation in politics, they bespoke "totalitarian democracy." Thus did Horowitz, the epigone as academic sociologist, accuse Tom Hayden, the epigone as political actor, of the worst possible sin: "Fascism returns in the United States not as a right-wing ideology, but almost as a quasi-leftist ideology, an ironic outcome that Sorel anticipated when in his own writings he celebrated Mussolini and Lenin as if they were really two peas in one pod."

■■■

Emerson argued that "representative men" extend two kinds of service. First, there is metaphysical and material aid, such that "the boy believes there is a teacher who can sell him wisdom." Eventually, the need for such aid tapers away, leaving indirect aid in the form of a "pictorial or representative quality" appealing chiefly to the intellect. In the late seventies and early eighties Irving Louis Horowitz continued to write regularly about C. Wright Mills, but his conclusions, and his tone, turned negative and sour. By 1983, when he published the first, and what remains the only full-scale biography, he had issued four volumes of essays containing nearly five hundred items. In 1969, Horowitz had moved from Washington University to Rutgers, where had become the Hannah Arendt Professor of Sociology, as well as the head of Transaction Publishers. His needs and ambitions amply gratified, he turned viciously against his benefactor.

Perhaps the best testimony against the image he contrived for Mills in the sixties was the completeness with which he abandoned it in the eighties. On page four of *C. Wright Mills: An American Utopian*, he reported a "near-unanimous negative consensus about him." The rest of the book went toward upsetting everything he had written previously. No longer a "true reformer," Mills was now a utopian. No longer a good academic, he was now "a prophet and fanatic." No longer a principled, noble man of personal integrity, he was now a canny operator who made use of the strategic and tactical resources surrounding him in order to advance his vainglory, before it destroyed him.

In "A Postscript to a Sociological Utopian," an essay presented at academic conferences and published in 1989, Horowitz deepened and extended these charges, slurring Mills as a "bigot." In the sixties, Horowitz had written: "Mills was one of that special breed of men who could be as comfortable in the Harlem ghetto looking up at Morningside Heights as in looking down from the Heights of Harlem. This flexibility of human character was his shield and his buckler." Now he claimed: "In C. Wright Mills I was dealing with a sadly flawed individual, a human being who had biased attitudes on many issues including minorities, Jews, women, and especially blacks."

The animus shifted. The form stayed the same. The chapter on Mills' intellectual debts Horowitz transposed wholesale from the introduction to *Sociology and Pragmatism*. The chapter on White Collar he transposed from his pamphlet for the R.D.M. Corporation. The chapter on Marxism he transposed from a scattering of Mills' early essays. Horowitz, moreover, still examined Mills' character and ideas exclusively through the context of the modern academic professional. In the sixties, he had used this context to make a martyr out of Mills, had claimed that only a collective misunderstanding on the part of the profession had obscured his natural qualification for the academic way. Now Horowitz said Mills had been "marginal and antiprofessional" all along. "It is correct to note," he wrote, "that Mills could no longer really be properly defined as being within the field of sociology; certainly he was not by the end of the decade." It was just because Horowitz still measured his subject by the norms of academic sociology that he still had a fractious character on his hands. More than two decades had passed, he noted in his introduction, and yet "my greatest difficulty was getting people who knew Mills to speak about him in a calm and reasoned manner." During interviews conducted for the biography "the sense of his presence so was imminent that old arguments were often rekindled rather than dampened at the mention of his name."

Still Horowitz disdained to generate falsifiable propositions with publicly available evidence by way of conscientious research. Most of the letters he cited in the biography referred to his private collection, not to the Mills archives at the University of Texas. Many of his textual interpretations referred readers to the translated essays in *De Hombres Sociales y Movimientos Politicos*. "A Postscript to a Sociological Utopian," where he aired the most damaging personal allegations, offered not so much as a scrap of evidence; not even an anecdote.

Moments of incoherence marred the new portrait as they had marred the old one. Early in the biography Horowitz transposed a formulation he had used in the introduction to *Sociology and Pragmatism*: "The thought of power did not intoxicate or absorb Mills. If anything the reverse was true: Mills was obsessed with the potential of reason to redirect the irrational rush of raw power. This is not Manichaeism, but old-fashioned rationalism." In "Postscript," he flatly contradicted himself: "Mills had abandoned the tensions of human interaction for a world of good and evil. He was possessed by a kind of Manichaeism, a poor substitute for pragmatism." The last sentence of the biography was a masterpiece of self-parody: "That America was Mills' essential laboratory for testing, teasing, and thundering was an accident of birth, but one which gave special meaning and a cutting edge, albeit a blunt one, to his search for the Fourth Epoch—the utopian longing within all ideologists and, I daresay, all sociologists."

And again, while some of the errors fell into no special pattern, most leaned in the same ideological direction. "Poor Mills was never able to live down his Texas background even though he had not the vaguest idea what to do with a gun or a horse," Horowitz wrote. Lewis Coser falsified the claim in the *American Journal of Sociology*: "Early in 1949, Mills and his wife Ruth moved into the house owned by David Riesman in Chicago, where my wife and I also lived while Riesman worked at Yale to complete *The Lonely Crowd*. On the day of Mills' arrival, we were shocked to hear gunshots suddenly coming from his apartment. Frantically rushing upstairs, we found that Mills had installed a cardboard target over the mantelpiece and was happily shooting at it."

Another kind of criticism surfaced in the *International Social Science Review*, where sociologist Don Martindale accused Horowitz of "borrowing" without attribution from his own writings: "Moreover, it is difficult to avoid the impression that too often Horowitz has provided hypothetical contexts for interpreting Mills' actions and ideas which supply only probable or possible connections and which may distort the reality. In the one period that I am acquainted with firsthand, Mills' Wisconsin years, I am aware of a number of omissions and distortions in Horowitz's account." Nobuko Gerth, the widow of Mills' longtime friend, accused Horowitz likewise in the *International Journal of Politics, Culture, and Society*. About one turning point in the relationship between Mills and Gerth, she wrote that "Horowitz's account of this incident is a fabrication."

On April 15, 1984, a letter from Mills' widow, his first wife, and his three children was published in the *New York Times Book Review*. The family reported finding "more than 50 errors of biographical fact" in *C. Wright Mills: An American Utopian*. Some of the errors concerned their own backgrounds and biographies. More seriously, the family's letter disputed a key sentence in Horowitz's preface: "I have tried to contact every living person who has firsthand information on Mills." The letter falsified the claim by pointing out that Horowitz "did not contact either family members or Mills' closest friends in connection with this book." Horowitz himself had met Mills "only twice."

Horowitz's reply, published a month later, shed little direct light on the dispute. He claimed that he had met Mills in 1951, when he was a graduate student in philosophy at Columbia. Subsequently, he claimed, he had met with Mills in West Nyack three times, not two, in addition to which he had spent time with him discussing the manuscript of *The Marxists*, Mills' last book. "Indeed, I say without fear of contradiction that no other single person was more important in assisting him on his last work. Mills himself acknowledged as much on several occasions."

As usual, what Horowitz did not say was most instructive. Challenged on a point of vested interest by those in the best position to undermine him, he did not describe himself as literary executor, as

Time reported, nor as one of Mills' "most brilliant students," as editors
at Oxford believed. What he did say, moreover, he said in such a way
as to discourage the possibility of testing the discrepancy between
these images and the image offered by the family. About the time and
place of the "several occasions" of assisting Mills on *The Marxists*, and
about the ostensible meeting in 1951, he said nothing concrete, and
thus, indeed, could have no "fear of contradiction," for contradictions
of fact arise only when contrary evidence exists to test the validity
of a disputed claim to truth. Horowitz said that most of the time he
had spent with Mills on the book took him outside the family's field
of vision, "for obvious professional reasons."

The acknowledgements page of *The Marxists*, the best evidence for
his claims, neither supported nor refuted them. Mills acknowledged
Horowitz without comment alongside eighteen other colleagues.
Given that Mills was speaking for himself in the one public forum
set aside for such things, Horowitz's reply to the family seems high-
handed. But then, having kicked the terms of the dispute into the
familiar vacuum of warrantless assertion, he went on the attack. He
dismissed rational grounds for the protest by indicating that the family
was trying to discredit him, though he did not offer any motive to
suggest why they might want to do so. The family's "ludicrous" letter
was "beyond comprehension," nothing more than "outrage served up
as intellectual pablum." Turning to address the widowed Yaroslava
Mills, to whom he had dedicated *Power, Politics, and People*, he boasted
that his relations with her late husband antedated hers. He had met
him (he claimed) in 1951, "considerably before she even knew the
name Mills." These matters well in hand, he rose to a grand finish:
"I shall not know, any more than I did 22 years ago, adjust uncomfortable truths to fit pleasant myths." Horowitz saluted himself for
having written "a work more widely heralded than any other written
about a sociologist." What it heralded, he did not say.

"Horowitz's book is a balanced, judicious intellectual biography,"
wrote Jackson Lears in the *Journal of American History*. Perhaps it
was the presumption of personal authority, cultivated by Horowitz
over many years, which caused responsible reviewers to turn in

flattering reviews. The dust jacket on the book did advertise him as "this country's preeminent authority on C. Wright Mills." Or perhaps it was the political mood of the early eighties, which afforded no kind of solicitude for the cultural heroes of the sixties. Then, too, no rivals had appeared. Although a handful of essays on Mills had appeared in the seventies and early eighties, the best biographical writing remained unpublished, in dissertations. For one reason or another, questions that should have been obvious went begging for answers.

If Mills really had been "beyond the professional pale," then how had Horowitz been able to persuade twenty-eight professional social scientists to honor him in *The New Sociology*? Why had Horowitz written there that "Mills was not the intellectual isolate he pictured himself to be"? If Mills really had purveyed pathological personal biases, then why had Horowitz, with his fund of intimate, truthful knowledge, neglected to report them in the sixties? Why had he insisted upon the opposite, writing on the second page of *Power, Politics, and People* that "his victory was both public and private"? In "Postscript," Horowitz called Mills "a human figure, the ordinary sort one sees about the Academy." Why did this belated discovery of humanity so startle Horowitz? Why had he once seen magic where he might have seen a man? Such questions were not asked, much less answered, by reviewers. Nor were they acknowledged by the author. Nowhere in debunking the mythos of Mills did Horowitz let on that it was he, more than anybody else, who had been responsible for creating it in the first place. Having once exaggerated Mills' virtues beyond recognition, he now exaggerated his vices, feeding on both ends of the corpse.

▌▌▌

Like Thorstein Veblen, who died in 1929, C. Wright Mills died at the dawn of a decade that seemed to vindicate his insights. In the decades that followed, however, neither the new sociologists nor the political intellectuals generated anything to compare with Joseph Dorfman's *Thorstein Veblen and His America* (1934), no common text to set forth a reliable body of knowledge in the absence of which informed disagreement miscarries. The literature surrounding Mills since 1962 still falls into a few camps that spar for the right to derive lessons from his biography. Accreditation is the main criteria raised in their disputes. Reputation-mongering seems to be the main point. Few intellectuals may stand up to the scrutiny of the culture wars, which demand from their heroes a mix of psychic security and ideological rectitude. All gestures of independence, being inconvenient, are greeted with suspicion. Herein lies the irony. "He didn't ask for intellectual allegiance, nor did he respect those who offered it too readily," E.P. Thompson noted of Mills.

Horowitz is the representative figure in the vexed story of Mills' afterlife, for all those introductions, prefaces, bibliographies, postscripts, essays, reviews, and remarks, if read straight through, entomb his memory in a chaos of "non-facts" and irreconcilable attributes. There are no possibilities for dialectical progress; no stable points of departure; nothing to begin with. How did Horowitz make such a conspicuous success out of such a preposterous failure? Part of the answer lies in the late twentieth-century transformation of the academic vocation. Neither "communities of the competent," in the liberal image, nor ideological expressions of class, in the Marxist image, academic groups in America operate as rackets whose symbolic and material resources are monopolized by petty cliques and bosses. The new class of professional social scientists that emerged in the late sixties and seventies professed to free themselves of the kind of debilitating political struggle practiced by their radical counterparts, while redirecting it into competencies attuned to success. Duly honored, the new class showed up in the eighties as a group of solipsistic superstar professors who taught everybody how very much could be done with so very little.

Horowitz, too, may stand for the strictly rational, unreflexive manner of valuation prominent in the social science research industry. This was the manner that Mills criticized in *The Sociological Imagination*, where he urged intellectual craftsmen to embrace "the ethics of scholarship" even if their institutions and professions had forgotten them. Scholarly ethics included "a developed carefulness and attention to detail, a habit of being clear, a skeptical perusal of alleged facts, and a tireless curiosity about their possible meanings, their bearings on other facts and notions." Perhaps, finally, Horowitz exposes the limits of the quest for positive knowledge in social science. Positivism claps up the disorderly actuality of modern experience into unreal antinomies, whereas biography may never be expected to choose between rationality or irrationality, science or politics, reason or passion. Horowitz claimed, plausibly, that *C. Wright Mills: An American Utopian* was "a work more widely heralded than any other written about a sociologist." The competition was paltry.

In October 2006, the Special Collections Division, Paterno Library, Penn State University, announced its acquisition of the "Irving Louis Horowitz/Transaction Publishers Archive." The press release said that among the items deposited by Horowitz were "papers of the late sociologist C. Wright Mills." Since the description goes no further, and since the collection is not yet open to the public, it is impossible to know which of Mills' papers Horowitz deposited. Nor is it possible to know whether money was paid out in the transposition. The Mills papers constitute "a highlight" of the collection, according to William Joyce, the head of Special Collections, who could say no more than this.

Knowing the details of the transposition may be beside the point. An archive bearing Horowitz's name and including original Mills papers is sure to perpetuate the ostensibly intimate connection between the two men, and this maneuver has been a recognizable method of advancement ever since Henry James's *The Aspern Papers* betrayed the ingenuity of epigones in the laundering of literary reputation. James also bared the therapeutic motive that creeps behind masks of beneficence. Sure enough, it shows here, in a letter written by Horowitz in 1961 as Mills convalesced from a heart attack. "While laid up in the hospital last week (empathy pains no doubt) I came across this 'letter to the editor' in the Rochester Democrat and Chronicle, commenting on your book. I felt certain you would like to see it, so here it is enclosed."

Irving Louis Horowitz has made a mess of Mills, but one thing he has not done is leave him alone. His many volumes, best approached as sociological equivalents to junk science, keep on coming. *The De-composition of Sociology* (1993) blamed "left-wing fascism" for spoiling the scientific aspirations of *The New Sociology*. A profile of Mills in *Tributes* (2004) recycled material from 1962, passed along old errors, and generated a fresh round of contradictions. The 2005 edition of *The Anarchists* offered "a final statement of support for Wright, fulfilling at least in part his intellectual legacy, and allowing for an appreciation of what his thinking meant in my own development." *Daydreams and Nightmares* (1990), Horowitz's most revealing book, describes his early years as an impoverished son of Jewish immigrants, a tough boy who speculated in petty crime while clawing his way out of the Harlem ghetto. Remarking on the "more than twenty years I spent in researching a biography of the late C. Wright Mills, entitled *An American Utopian*," he said "I discovered that much of what I knew about myself figured in the writing of this book." What he discovered he did not say.

ACKNOWLEDGEMENTS

A portion of "HISTORY AS VOCATION" first appeared as "All the Privileged Must Have Prizes" in *Times Higher Education* (July 10, 2008): 42, 44.

"THE HITCHENS EFFECT" first appeared as "Journalists or Defenders of the Faith?" in *Free Inquiry*, volume 18, Spring 1998.

"THE TOUGHEST JOB" first appeared as "Writing Teachers of America Unite!" in *culturefront*, volume 8, Summer 1999.

"GRADUATE ECONOMICS" first appeared in the *Washington Post Magazine*, April 9, 2000.

"NOAM CHOMSKY AND ACADEMIC HISTORY" first appeared in *Counterpunch*, January 8/9, 2005.

"THE END OF SOCIOLOGY?" first appeared in the *Boston Review*, volume 28, December 2003/January 2004.

"JAMES AGEE, THE ANARCHIST SUBLIME" first appeared in *The Gettysburg Review*, volume 20, number 4, Winter 2007.

"WHAT HAPPENED TO SEX SCANDALS?" first appeared in the *Journal of American History*, volume 87, December 2000. Reprinted by permission of the Organization of American Historians. "PITY WARREN HARDING" first appeared as a pair of letters to the editor of the *Journal of American History*, volume 88, June 2001. Reprinted by permission of the Organization of American Historians.

"A NOTE ON ANTI-AMERICANISM" first appeared in *New Politics*, volume 12, Summer 2008.

"REMEMBERING RICHARD HOFSTADTER" first appeared as "The Quiet Center" in the *New York Observer*, June 19, 2006.

"PERSONAL PRAGMATISM" first appeared as an untitled review in the *Boston Review*, volume 26, October/November 2001.

"INFORMATION JUNKIES" first appeared as "Seduced by Information" in *The Chronicle Review*, volume 54, number 31, April 11, 2008.

"THE BIG DISCOURSE" first appeared in *The Nation*, volume 271, October 9, 2000.

"THE DECIDERS" first appeared in the *New York Times Book Review*, May 14, 2006.

"NO-MAN'S-LAND" first appeared in *Penultimate Adventures with Britannia: Personalities, Politics, and Culture in Britain*, edited by Wm. Roger Louis. London: I.B. Tauris, 2008.

"THE EPIGONE'S EMBRACE" first appeared in the *Minnesota Review*, number 68, Spring 2007.

Another book from John H. Summers:
The Politics of Truth: Selected Writings of C. Wright Mills, selected and introduced by John H. Summers and published by Oxford University Press, 2008. ISBN-13: 9780195343045, ISBN-10: 0195343042

1704141

Made in the USA